Expecting the Unexpected

seeking the silver linings …

Expecting the Unexpected

seeking the silver linings …

by

Harpreet Kaur

Table of Contents

A letter to my greatest gifts, my Arjun and Saajan;

I contemplated whether to ever publish my journey in fear of causing you both even a drop of pain, but I hope that by actually sharing this, it will help other women feel less lonely, and, in turn, you'll be able to see that speaking up and going against the grain can be a positive thing and that there is no shame in sharing our struggles. Please know that when you get to some of the difficult chapters, this is no longer how I feel today.

I'm not sure if you'll ever choose to read this book, but if you do, before you start, please ensure you have enough time to read right to the end because it's a journey. There may be some things that are difficult to read, but also many moments when mummy had breakthroughs—I hope you are able to focus on those breakthroughs and feel proud and know that you can achieve anything that you put your minds to! Life is all about how we choose to view it.

I love you both more than words can express. You have shaped me to be the woman that I am today. I am so grateful for the journey of motherhood that I have been allowed to experience with you both—what an honour it is to be your mum. I love you so much.

Yours always, Mummy x

Acknowledgements

Writing a book is harder than I thought and more rewarding than I could have ever imagined. Rather ironically, the editing of this book has taken place at the very hospital that many of the events I share took place at. It has been the most surreal experience… but I'll save that story for another day… perhaps in another book!

Since I started Baby Brain Memoirs, I have had the pleasure of connecting with many of you that have chosen to follow our journey. A heartfelt thank you for joining us on this rollercoaster, for supporting me, for being open to learning and for carrying me through some of my darkest days. You will never know how grateful I am to you for being a part of my story and for allowing me to be a part of yours by sharing your stories.

Whilst Baby Brain Memoirs has given a glimpse in to our lives, I hope that this book will give you a peak behind closed doors.

I want my book to be a lifeline to women just like me; suffering alone—plagued by unwanted thoughts, and terrified of sharing their truth through fear of judgement in our community. I wanted my journey documented in one place so you can pick this book up and ride the journey with me, and know that you are not alone and that it *is* going to be okay.

A big thank you to Preetam for being the rock of our family and for holding us together despite the hurdles we've faced through life. I think it's safe to say we can pretty much accomplish anything together! Your hard work, determination and commitment to us is second to none and we love you so much. We haven't had the easiest ride, but I'm glad I get to do it all with you!

Arjun and Saajan, you have taught me to love like I've never loved before. It has been quite the journey with both of you and I wouldn't change it for the world—you are my happy! Thank you for being my greatest strength always.

A huge heartfelt thank you to our families for being there unconditionally, for holding us up when we had no strength and for reminding us that we will always have an army of support. There are no real words to express my gratitude or to describe the comfort that provides me.

Thank you to Amrit and Sav for being my outlet, my escape, for never giving up on me and for encouraging me to write this book. To Dina for stepping in when I felt I couldn't with Saajan. Your bond with him is so special and I'm so grateful for your love and support.

Thank you to the NHS and the Royal Brompton and Harefield Hospital Trusts for being such a big part of our story. The love and care shown by the midwives, nurses, doctors, consultants and support staff made all the difference through some of the tougher days whilst also taking care of us!

And last but not least, my deepest gratitude to our Down's syndrome family for taking me out of my darkest hole, holding my hand tight and never breaking your promise.

Thank you to everyone that has been a part of our journey!

With love,
Harps x

Introduction

IT WAS 2000. I WAS 15 and I could sense that things were tough for my parents. I very clearly remember Christmas; our home was filled with warmth and joy despite my parents not having enough money for a Christmas tree, let alone gifts. My memory isn't a sad one though—I remember making paper chains with my sisters and decorating a floor plant instead of a Christmas tree. The sight of the paper chains on the plant is something that has always stayed with me. I think from a very young age, I learnt that joy didn't come from "stuff"; it came from the people around you. However, I do recall getting myself in a bit of a tizz about how my sisters were not neatly gluing the chains!

Since I was a kid, I've always been a bit of an over-reactor; I wear my drama queen crown with pride! Haha! I've always been the vivacious family-orientated sort; the kind that is a bit of a bookworm and nailed my exams but isn't not necessarily that street smart. I unintentionally came fifth in the world in one of my professional accounting exams but wouldn't have a clue how to navigate my way around the London Underground without a bit (a lot) of assistance! I was the type who never gave in to the social pressures of looking "cool" and, until the age of 18, I quite enjoyed being dropped at school by my parents or granddad (who many mistook to be my dad as he pulled up outside school with his shades and leather jacket on!) whereas others may have been slightly embarrassed! I am an accountant by trade but creative by nature—you can only get so creative with Excel! The sort who hopes to leave the person I'm with feeling a sense of lightness after spending time with me (maybe not physically, though, as I'm a feeder!). I am a passionate person who sometimes finds it difficult to mask my true feelings—the double-edged sword. It's the thing that those who are close to me love about me, but the thing that gets me into trouble the most! I care about having deep and meaningful relationships but sometimes bear the weight of the world on my shoulders—an emotional sponge. I have a bit of a short fuse at the best of times and have been Little Miss Bossy Boots from a young age (I tried to teach my sisters algebra when they were six!). Yet, I'm also the type that gets shit done. My friends call me the girl next door—I would much rather curl up on the sofa with a good chick flick than don a whistle and rave until the early hours! I love Nutella and clouds. Party planning is my passion.

That pretty much sums me up! At 34 years of age, most of that still stands, except I drive myself around now! Haha!

Being one of three girls, I've always been really close to my family. Growing up, my sisters and I fought lots over clothes and shoes but protected each other so fiercely if anyone tried to "start" on any one of us. My sisters are twins. Harveer (Harv) and Gurveer (Goov), are six years younger than me and sometimes the age gap has meant that I've acted more like a mother figure (their words not mine!). Figuratively, I refer to them as my pillars of support—no matter what life throws our way, we know we have each other and the comfort I take from that is huge. It's true that the best gift you could give a girl is a sister. I got extra lucky!

I've always admired other sister relationships where there appears to be unconditional openness, peace and harmony. It always felt a little bit different to ours which has always been full of chaos! Full of love but also fire, compassion but also annoyance, laughter and also tears. I blame the Taurus in all three of us!

Growing up, while we were close, we didn't share every gory detail of our lives with each other—perhaps it was the age difference and them feeling fearful of my reaction to certain things. Perhaps I held back from sharing as I felt like I needed to shield them from grown-up stuff. As we've gotten older, and as we've experienced trials and tribulations through life, we are a lot more open with each other, and, at times, probably over-share (I'll spare you the deets!)! In hindsight, I wish I'd been a little more approachable but you live and learn—it's something that influences my parenting with my kids now.

Interestingly, being a "single" sibling to twin sisters has sometimes meant I've questioned my place. They'd often take "twin selfies" or do "twin things" and I'd feel self-conscious about where I stood, unbeknown to them. I've always found their relationship so fascinating—despite having shared a womb, I admire their unique differences, both in likes and dislikes, as well as their opinions and outlook on life.

As our relationships have matured, we value and appreciate each other's different personalities and, I think, we balance each other out pretty well. Each of us serves a very different yet beautiful purpose in our sistership.

I've always resumed the role of the elder protective child—in the South Asian community, perhaps the stereotypical view of what a son or brother may do. My dad always lovingly referred to us as his "love loves" growing up; even in his phone book, we are stored as e.g., "Harps Love Love". He's always been loving and affectionate towards us; his bear hugs provide the same comfort today as they did when we were little! He thinks about us in everything he does. When we were little, as "little" as 16, after a long day's work, he'd often come home with three Kinder Eggs—one for each of us. We'll always be his little girls even though I have my own children now!

My dad is my greatest inspiration. His demeanour is calm and he has a very peaceful aura. He has the hugest heart and a humble nature. I could tell you a few stories which show his kindness, but I'll share my favourite of them all! In 2014, while my mum's sister was in India on holiday with my uncle, she sat in a taxi and spotted a small picture of my father on the dashboard. Baffled, she asked, "Excuse me, sir, how do you know my brother-in-law and why do you have a picture of him on your dashboard?!" The gentleman replied, "Ma'am, this man is someone who changed my life. When he visited India in 2012, as I was driving him to Delhi, we spoke for hours and hours about our families. I shared with him some of my struggles, then this man helped me to buy a new vehicle so I could make more money to support my family. With a new car, I am able to get more business and it is more reliable. I am forever indebted to him." My father had never shared this with us. This story sums him up—he's one of the most selfless, kind and humble humans I know—but maybe I'm biased!

Dad quotes the best analogies to make a point and they always make sense. Given my fiery personality (that's putting it mildly!), my favourite of his is, "A matchstick has to burn itself before it burns anything else", when referring to anger. He has the most giving heart, is full of knowledge and wisdom and always has time and patience for others. Growing up with four women, I guess he mastered the latter pretty well!

He's always been free-spirited—perhaps losing his mum at the age of nine made him value the gift of life early on. He's really adventurous—some of his slightly crazy antics include an eight-week hitch-hiking trip in his early twenties in America, travelling from New York to Los Angeles and on to Las Vegas. He made it into the Bennington Banner, a local newspaper in the US, when a reporter for the newspaper spotted him on the roadside at 7 am. The newspaper clipping is like a trophy for his adventure which he's super proud of! It's clear to see the excitement he feels when he animatedly shares stories with us from the trip. Growing up, my sisters and I would scoot around a coffee table as he cut us fruit lovingly whilst we eagerly listened to him as he animatedly shared stories with us from the trip. We'd always be left in awe of his antics! One of my favourite stories—oblivious to the on-goings of the world, he decided to go for a swim in the sea at Redondo Beach in California. Arriving at the beach, he thought, "Wow! I have the entire beach to myself!" Moments later, he almost got wiped out by a tidal wave!—he didn't get the memo!

That's my dad—always taking risks and living to tell the tale! He's a firm believer in "what will be, will be"—destiny and all that! Us girls have always struggled to battle with him on finding an equilibrium between his belief and tempting fate!

My dad has always been my go-to in any tricky situation and he's always there encouraging us to strive for our dreams. He hosts tours of the local Gurdwara (Sikh temple) which is one of the largest in the world outside of India, Sri Guru Singh Sabha Southall. His audiences range from children in primary school to university students from all around the world. He has received hundreds of letters afterwards which echo my sentiments. He's humble, accepting and forgiving and is who I aspire to be like. He explains things in a loving and composed manner and I'm always in awe of how he

Passing through

Brown

Parmjit Virdi, 22, a native of Amritsar, Punjab, India, and a student of law at Nottingham University in Kent, England passed through South Shaftsbury this morning on the last leg of his eight week tour of the United States. Virdi has never been to this country before. He said he has found Americans friendly and open. "Americans enjoy life. They have a good life," he said, though he admitted "It's been rough out hthere." He headed west from New York City seven weeks ago, took a northerly route to Denver, Colo., stopped at Las Vegas where he lost $10 and won $4, proceeded to Los Angeles, dipped down to Baja, California, then backtracked, went north to San Francisco, returning east across Canada. "Hollywood, switchboard" is written on the left hand side of his weathered map of the United States. He said he was told when he got to L.A. to go to Hollywood and call "the switchboard" and he would get a room. He did. The pockets of his tightly packed knapsack are overflowing with tickets and brochures. One from Knott's Berry Farm in Los Angeles fell out as he was looking for his notebook. In that book he had written the lyrics of Punjabi folk songs, which he sings, accompanying himself with sablas drums, which he carries in his sack. He also plays the sitar, but it is too delicate to carry, he said.

The Bennington Banner newspaper article from my dad's hitchhiking adventures in America!

7

manages to stay calm even in the craziest of situations! I wish I'd inherited more of those calm genes!

My mum is the baby of six siblings and is definitely the most pampered! She has a thing about pockets, makes the best tandoori paneer (Indian cheese) and dhaal (curried lentils) and has an eye for Indian fashion! She even designed my wedding outfit. She is the queen of organisation and buying new mug sets! My mum's faith in God is second to none. She has been waking up at 2 am religiously since the age of 16 to do her prayers before heading to the Gurdwara at 4 am. I am always left in awe of her dedication. Even at the age of almost 60, she is so committed to her routine and her love for the Almighty.

You know you have that one person in your life that you speak to and you instantly feel like everything is going to be okay? Yep, that's my mum for me. My mother has always been my best friend. I lean on her for the strength and comfort that only she can provide me. No matter how old I grow, the comfort I take in her reassurance and advice is second to none. She's never been one to mollycoddle us or feed into any insecurities. Instead, she's always there to challenge any negative beliefs.

I remember very vividly the day of my Anand Karaj (Sikh wedding ceremony). I was very nervous before walking into the temple before the ceremony and asked my cousin to call my mum who was sitting in the main procession hall. Expecting to share an emotional moment with her before I took this leap of faith, she did the opposite and told me to buckle up and get myself in there! As much as that wasn't the reaction I was expecting, I appreciate her rational view on things—her life advice has been invaluable and I have so much faith and trust in her judgement. I believe her prayers have provided us with a protective shield and carried us through life at some of our toughest times. I take hope and courage from my mum. I've always been able to confide in her without fearing her reaction, even when I knew that sometimes she'd be disappointed in my choices! I've been able to share some of my biggest secrets with my mother, and, for that, I'm grateful. It's something that doesn't always feature in South Asian mother-daughter relationships!

The older I become, the more I realise how truly blessed I am to have the parents that I do. They have provided us with a solid foundation. They have continually provided us with guidance and boundaries but never suffocated us and would always be there to hold our hand if we wanted to try something new, but equally, they would keep us in check if need be. Unlike the stereotypical view of Asian girls being brought up in very strict environments, I never felt the need to escape from our childhood home; I always preferred being at home over going out as it has always been a warm and comforting environment. Our parents have always been our greatest cheerleaders, supporting us in whatever endeavours we have chosen to dip our toes into and have always celebrated us, no matter how big or small our achievements, however, we never had the parental pressure to be high achievers academically to become doctors or lawyers like many of our friends did!

Our childhood consisted of:

- Grabbing a 99p flake ice cream from Mcdonald's and going for long evening drives after dinner at least once a week.
- Often dining out as a family at our local favourite eatery.
- Dedicating our Saturday nights to watching TV with the family—*Gladiators*, Bruce's Forsyth's *The Price is Right* followed by *Blind Date*
- Spending our Saturday afternoons making French bread pizza while watching *FBI Files*. My dream job at that time was to be an FBI agent—maybe in another life if I'm born an American citizen! I still love watching any sort of crime documentary!

My family

It wasn't all a bed of roses though; I very vividly remember facing hardships as a family too—like the paper chains at Christmas. But those memories aren't filled with the hardships but more with the resilience and faith that my parents showed.

Being born into the Sikh faith, we'd frequently host religious functions where we had kirtan (sung religious hymns), bringing people together and where we were frequently told Sikh history stories which provided us with invaluable lessons. The Gurdwara has always been my safe haven. Sikhism is more a way of life than anything for me. Though I may not be a baptised Sikh, my faith is what has got me through life thus far.

Around the age of 16, I got my first "proper" job working at Currys, an electronics store, as a cashier. My ideal job was to work on the checkout at Tesco but this was close enough! Here, I met Amrit. I've always found Amrit so endearing—how she's always stood by her beliefs. At Currys, the workforce was predominantly male but Amrit never let that intimidate her. She has the most beautiful immaculate silky hair and a magical smile where her eyes twinkle! I often find myself reminiscing about the good old Currys days when our biggest worry was what we would eat for lunch! Ours is a friendship that is still going strong 18 years later.

It was around this time I also met Sav. Sav is feisty but loving, she wears her heart on her sleeve and is so passionate about the things she believes in. Like me, she too has two sisters (and two brothers!) and we often find commonalities—namely, being the elder bossy sister in our respective homes! Since I met Sav, I'd say we've spent longer periods of our lives speaking to each other daily than not! We live perhaps 10 minutes away from each other but we barely see each other; it's a friendship that doesn't require much face-to-face interaction and the low maintenance side of it makes it even more beautiful! Like Amrit, Sav has always challenged my thoughts and plays devil's advocate in any given situation—something I value in both of my besties.

As I mentioned, my aspirations as a young girl weren't your typical ones. I wanted to work on the tills in Tesco. I didn't intend on going to university but the Head of Sixth Form called me into his office and convinced me to at least apply. I was so careless with my UCAS form as I wasn't at all interested in the idea of going to university. I attended a local University of London merely because I didn't fancy living out and nor did I fancy figuring out the trains and tubes! I handed in my dissertation a week early—I'm THAT girl—and somehow managed to get a first in my degree! I went on to work in Finance—not something that I had planned but something that felt "safe" in case of a recession. A wise decision, I'd later learn!

CHAPTER 1:

A Fairy Tale…

Growing up, like many girls, I had a picture of what my life would be when I was older. Naïve, perhaps, but always the dreamer. Like most little girls, I dreamt of meeting my Prince Charming (I also encountered many frogs along the way!).

Interestingly, many South Asian girls are discouraged from having boyfriends, but when it comes to the "marital" age (I'd say 20+), suddenly you're expected to whip out a potential husband from somewhere!

Preetam (aka Heera) is my real-life superman. He's hard-working, open-minded, wise beyond his years, has his priorities right and I always knew he'd make an incredible father. As we grow in our marriage, we appreciate the similarities we have. We both pick spending the evening at home watching a movie over a heavy night out and we're both driven and complement each other so well with our business acumen and approach to finances. Neither of us drinks alcohol, we are both early risers (even before we had kids!), we both love a good holiday and we both always think we're right, haha! Don't get me wrong, we also have our differences—I'm a social butterfly, and he's a bit more of a wallflower! He's a superbike-riding adrenaline junkie, whereas I'd rather hold everyone's jackets at a theme park! We both live in trackies but I sometimes like to dress up—he can't think of anything worse! His language of love is acts of service (I am truly spoilt with his breakfast creations!) whereas mine is words of affirmation. Like all, our marriage has had its fair share of challenges along the way. Marriage is very much a journey and, as you grow and evolve as individuals, so does the dynamic of your relationship.

The story of how Preetam (aka Heera) and I got together is quite an eventful one.

One sunny day, my sisters had been to the house of a family friend for her 18th birthday. When they got home, they said "OMG, Harps, you have to see their cousin!".

"Yeah, whatever", replied a rather cocky 20-year-old Harps.

Two months later, we were invited to another gathering at our family friend's house. This time, we all went.

We were sitting enjoying our traditional Indian snacks of samoseh and pakoreh—commonly featured at these types of gatherings. Often a source of conversation between aunties who have children above the age of 20, Preetam's mum said, "Does Harpreet have anyone?" Without asking directly, it was understood what this meant.

"Nehi, tusi daso je koi jaanda? (No; will you tell us if you know anyone?)" said my mum.

"I'd look no further than my own son", she replied behind her signature cheeky grin.

"Wow, I like her—she's so direct", I thought. But to be honest, I was young and a bit of a know-it-all at the time. I wasn't looking to settle down.

Preetam arrived.

"WOW, he's stunning!" I thought.

"Harpreet, this is Heera", said his mum. Heera was her affectionate name for him (translates to diamond) which I've adopted from her.

"Hi" he said shyly.

"Hi" I replied. And that was that.

"There's no way he doesn't have a girlfriend. He won't be interested in me anyway so I can stop fretting about giving an answer." This was something that I'd previously had to do with other rishteh (potential marriage proposals). I must admit, it was probably the first time I was stopped in my tracks—"He's soft on the eye, his parents and my parents get along so well, we are super-close to his cousins, he has a good job and our families seem so alike." He ticked many of the "boxes" that many South Asian girls have on their list.

The next day, while I was on my laptop on MSN Messenger catching up with school friends (if you're from the same generation as me—you'll know all about MSN Messenger! For those of you that aren't, it's kind of like a computer-based version of What's App!), and there popped up a friend request—PREETAM. I literally jumped off my bed!

"OMG! HE'S ADDING ME!?"

The year that followed consisted of me resisting Preetam's advances. (I still have the card that he sent me on Valentine's Day with a dozen red roses!). Eventually, we went our separate ways. I'd met my fair share of idiots on my journey so was always apprehensive. It almost felt too good to be true and so I was very resistant and fearful of being let down… again.

When we stopped talking, I'd often think about him and whether I'd let the perfect opportunity pass…

He met someone, I met someone and our paths divided.

Though Preetam and I didn't get together, what was born was a beautiful friendship between his sister, Mané, and I. We became closer than ever, saw each other at least four or five times a week and spoke constantly throughout our day. She became my very best friend; another sister. She was kind and funny and I enjoyed being in her company. Mané sometimes mentioned the idea of Preetam and I getting together, although, at this point, he and I had lost contact.

As the years passed and I matured (!), and circumstances changed for us both, Preetam and I reconnected (thank God for MSN!) and over time, it became obvious that we were chatting far more often than just friends would! We started as a long-distance relationship—Preetam was working on a project in Shanghai and the early stages of "us" was heavily reliant on Skype and dial-up internet (DSL). I remember frantically trying to mask the sound of the loud dial-up tone from my parents at ridiculous o'clock due to the time difference—heaven forbid they caught me talking to a boy in the middle of the night! I'd spend time getting ready before each Skype chat like I would for a date, ensuring my hair was in place and my lip gloss was on—that was me getting dressed up. I didn't own any other make-up till after I got married. My attire was always a tracksuit of some sort—I'd always owned more pairs of joggers than any other item of clothing!

Preetam moved back after a few months of us getting to know each other (with my guard down!). We were so excited for our first Christmas together and just being able to spend time with each other. Christmas has always been a warm and fuzzy time for us as it's a chance for us to be a family and I was excited to spend part of it with Preetam!

But life had something else in store and my excitement quickly turned to worry.

23rd December—Mum had been in bed for several days now. She hadn't woken up at 2 am and gone to the temple at 4 am as she had religiously done for as long as I could remember. It felt uncomfortable—something wasn't right.

We decided to call an ambulance although she resisted and pleaded with us not to (I forgot to mention how incredibly tenacious my beautiful mama can be!). Upon arrival, the paramedics checked mum in the ambulance. It felt like hours but moments later, they told us she needed to be taken to hospital. Frantic and in tears as I feared the worst, I called Preetam. He headed straight over and the moment he arrived, everything felt a little calmer. We headed straight to the hospital to meet my mum and

Goov. As we got to them, Goov told us that my mum had had an unexpected heart attack. Harv and I burst into uncontrollable tears while Goov stayed rational—she's always been the calmer one, the more logical one and the matter-of-fact one. We were terrified.

I felt lost, disconnected—my greatest strength was no longer able to be MY strength while we needed to be hers. Preetam rose to the situation and held us all together as my mum recovered in hospital.

He wasn't about to let Christmas be ruined. On Christmas Day, Preetam arrived at the hospital dressed in a red tracksuit, with a red sack containing our Christmas presents from home armed with an entire Christmas dinner that his mum had lovingly prepared. We were all so overwhelmed and in tears with the generosity and how thoughtful he and his family were. I was always told I'll just know when I meet the one—I knew at that moment he was indeed the one.

So, our story was quite an eventful one but one that has always cemented our belief that we were meant to be together.

Thankfully, my mum was okay, and, after surgery, was feeling much better. My mum's heart attack brought Preetam and I even closer. We felt like we'd been together for ages because of the intense experience. We both made it quite obvious that we were in this for the long haul and our parents knew. It's very common in our culture for the parents to be involved when talks of marriage arise to plan wedding dates and formalities, even before a proposal!

A few months later, Preetam proposed to me. Many girls may prefer a more romantic story of the Eiffel Tower or a surprise helicopter as part of their proposal but our proposal story was so "us"! It was a few weeks after Christmas and we were on our way to view a house to potentially purchase. As we pulled up outside the house, he asked if I'd like to pull a Christmas cracker. In hindsight, this was quite random given it was after Christmas, and also, why did he even have a Christmas cracker in his car? I said, "Sure", I pulled it and out came a little slip of paper (which I still have!) that said, "OPEN THE GLOVE BOX" and in the glove box was my ring. "Will you marry me, Harpsy Harpsy? x" read the note. As I sat there in my attire of choice—jogging bottoms and messy hair up, my eyes welled up as I said, "Yes!! Of course, I will!" Selfies weren't a thing then, not for me anyway, so we didn't even capture the memory but I'm glad I kept the little slip of paper as a memento!

Some may say we got engaged really quickly, but for us, having been in each other's lives for over four years on and off by this point, we had seen each other's good, bad and ugly (mostly anyway!).

I'd love to tell you that it was a fairy-tale and that it came without challenges but we had our fair share!

CHAPTER 2:

Happily Ever After… Sort Of

A<small>S EXCITED AS OUR PARENTS</small> were, some of the differences surfaced as we began speaking about wedding arrangements. Our social circle is large in comparison to Preetam's family who have maintained a modest one. Where my parents were happy to go along with whatever Preetam and I wanted, Preetam's parents were very much of the school of thought that the parents should decide. So, there were a few hurdles and compromises along the way!

I'm not going to pretend it was all plain sailing and that everyone was happy to see us together. We most definitely faced some resistance from extended family for reasons I'm still unsure of today! Being an overthinker, this wasn't healthy.

Through it all, Preetam held my hand tight. He showed me that together, we would be okay. I never had to ask for reassurance; it was always there. He's always made me feel safe and I've always felt that together, we can achieve absolutely anything. I'm grateful now for the resistance we faced back then as it pushed us even closer together, something that I wish I'd been wiser to back then.

I'm not entirely sure what made us choose, but we ended up deciding on a destination wedding in Goa. Preetam was such a gentleman when it came to wedding plans—that or he just wasn't fussed with the detail! I worked alongside a wedding planner, literally planning my wedding via an Excel spreadsheet!

As much as I knew in my heart of hearts that Preetam was the one for me, my enthusiasm and excitement were often dampened as I became laced with fear for what my future as a married girl would look like. It's a fear that many South Asian women have due to the stereotypical hardship that we sometimes hear of within the community. It didn't feel like I was being welcomed with open arms by everyone in the family. There were very obvious but unsaid qualms. My emotions were tangled at the time— the thought of leaving the warmth, security and love of my parents, especially after my mum's heart attack, the panic around if I'd be good enough, worrying about if I'd fit in and if I'd be treated well by *everyone*, dealing with change and obviously the most pressing question, "how would I go for a poo in their house?!"—It all felt somewhat overwhelming. What would my life be like?

My constant rock was my Heera.

Preetam and my dad especially got on like a house on fire as their business acumen and approach to life are so similar. I haven't met anyone else like Preetam of our generation. Even before we got together, he resumed a very caring role towards my sisters. My mum loved him from the get-go. For me, that meant everything given how close I am to my family. The final seal of approval came from our family dog, Chico, our fluffy and fiery Westie (rest in eternal peace in doggy heaven, Chico), who pretty much would've licked Preetam to death given the chance! I really trusted Chico's intuition.

I also frequently visited Preetam's family house to become familiar with my new home, though I felt anxious every time I did. I'd never lived outside of my parents' home; I'd even lived at home for university so this was a pretty big change and unchartered territory for me.

My mother-in-law always greeted me with open arms and the question on her lips was always, "What would you like to eat?"—something she still asks every time we visit even today! Visiting there eased my anxiety a little as I felt a little more at home. It was always very casual—there were no pretences around what I had to wear or what I looked like. Being a teacher, Preetam's mum is pretty cool to hang out with. I enjoyed spending time with her, and, in years to come, their home would become my sanctuary.

Preetam and I had our beautiful wedding in February 2012 where we were surrounded by family and friends celebrating the most beautiful time of our lives—full of colour, food and laughter with the beautiful backdrop of Mother Nature and her ocean. Considering there was no alcohol, our parties were pretty wild and our crazy family managed to even break the dance floor at one of the pre-functions! But still, I felt the distance and the coldness from a few in the family that I was about to be married into. It wasn't quite how I'd imagined my wedding build-up to be as a little girl. Thankfully, the celebrations far outweighed any worries in that regard—I was able to focus on the fact that this wasn't only our wedding, it was also a giant family holiday full of memories.

Our wedding reception in beautiful Goa

It was Preetam's vadi masi's (auntie—mum's sister) last-ever holiday as she sadly passed away six weeks later. The time I got to spend with her after our wedding in Goa is ingrained in my heart; the pearls of wisdom that she shared with me ring in my ears whenever I'm faced with hardship—"In one ear and out the other, Harpreet." Her loving and sensible advice echoes in my ears frequently.

As I danced the night away at my wedding celebrations, I was blissfully unaware of the complexities of being a grown-up and how our personal life would pan out. I liked being blissfully unaware. I liked being a dreamer.

Upon our arrival back from Goa, I dreaded going back to Preetam's house. I felt scared and anxious as the pretty sunsets and bright colours disappeared and as the reality of being a married woman sunk in.

"Hello! Welcome home!" cheered Preetam's mum as we entered.

Much to my relief, as soon as they opened the front door, I was greeted by the warm and inviting faces of my mother-in-law, father-in-law and Mané. I felt the pressure ease instantly from my shoulders and let out a sigh of relief.

There were no formalities—the first thing my mother-in-law said to me when I arrived at my new home was, "My own children don't wake up at a set time, so you don't have to either. This is your house as much as it is mine."

My in-laws have been far from the traditional in-laws portrayed on the Indian soap channel, *Star Plus*, thankfully! They have always been incredibly loving and supportive of me and from the moment I got married, I've felt very much at home in their house. We've always worked collaboratively and they've always treated me as a valued member of the family.

Interestingly, though my parents never spoke badly about mother-in-law/daughter-in-law relationships, perhaps because my mum hadn't been exposed to one, the South Asian culture very much presents a mother-in-law being there to simply pass judgement instead of someone that you could potentially form a loving relationship with. Many Indian soaps sensationalise the negative nature of mothers-in-law in that they'd have expectations of their daughters-in-law and also feel as though they were possessions that they could control.

Thankfully, my life doesn't mimic that of an Indian soap! My mother-in-law reminds me so much of my sister Harv—pretty sure they were mother and daughter in a previous life! She is life and soul of the party, unfiltered and such a cheerful character. She was centre stage at all of our wedding celebrations and her beautiful smile is a true reflection of her soul; she's always so happy for others. Don't get me wrong, we've had our ups and downs, but on the whole, we have a very healthy relationship.

From the start, we've been very open with each other but also respectful and the manner in which we converse is from a mutual understanding perspective. While they're traditional in some ways, for example, holding superstitious beliefs such as wearing black is bad luck, they're also incredibly modern. While I always dreamt of living in a joint family, my mother-in-law lovingly advised us to get our own place. As much as I knew it hurt her to encourage us to move out, she was setting her son free. She explained to us that the complexities of life and having pressured jobs meant that space was important for our marriage to flourish. She always taught me that before anything comes our marriage, then our children, then everyone else—something I value so much as I've heard horror stories about over-interfering mothers-in-law! She's full of wisdom and her easy-going and no-grudge attitude reminds me of my dad. I hope to adopt her nature when and if I'm a mother-in-law too!

My father-in-law is a man of few words—a little like Preetam. He's most famous for his love of coconut oil and apple cider vinegar as a remedy to cure most things! I admire his love for my mother-in-law's family and how he goes out of his way to ensure everyone is okay—again, something that isn't often seen in traditional Indian families and something that I believe Preetam has learnt from his father. Preetam's eyes often well up when we speak about his dad—since a young age, Preetam has followed his dad and learnt all of his trades like a sponge, from electrical work to woodwork.

Both of Preetam's parents centre their entire world around their family—something that you can feel on entering their home. There is the same warmth and comfort there as I experience in my own parents' home.

I enjoyed being a newlywed; I'd spend the days with my mother-in-law and Mané and would look forward to cosying up in bed to Preetam to watch a movie in the evenings. Though Mané and I had drifted apart over the last year, I was thankful that we were able to pick up where we'd left off and I felt like I had another sister again.

I didn't feel out of place in my new family; it felt like an extension of my own. My brother-in-law, Indy, shares my love for food and our days would often be centred around it (not much has changed!)—I've always enjoyed a good laugh with him. He loves a good prank, will always make light of a situation and lighten the mood and his ability to consume endless amounts of ice cream and popcorn still fascinates me!

Though I mentioned our families are similar, some of the differences I really value are how softly and sweetly they speak in Preetam's house. I also really value that my father-in-law is happy to get involved with the cooking and cleaning, roles often associated with females in our culture. I mentioned how unruly the twins and I were sometimes, but that wasn't really something I witnessed often at Preetam's house and the more time I spent there, the more I realised this is how I wanted my own family home to look—calm!

Though Preetam isn't really the outwardly emotional type, I've always admired his protectiveness over his parents. We are so similar in nature when it comes to our love for both sets of parents—whether it be wanting them to be with us on family holidays or ensuring they are at all our birthday celebrations to cut a cake the same way we did when we were little kids! Preetam and I have always treated each other's parents like our own. I don't take this for granted. I know we've had our fair share of hurdles, so I'm grateful that family bickering isn't something that features in our marriage! Our parents have always worked together to support us and to guide us.

In Indian families, often having a son is considered protection. My mum got a lot of slack for it when she had us—especially when she had the twins. It was almost mourned. Preetam always acknowledged that we don't have a brother without saying it by resuming many of the traditional roles a son would perhaps be expected to do. This is something that has been precious to me; I believe it's a value that his mother has instilled in him.

I think many women assume that moving into your own house after marriage is an escape from the realms of living with in-laws, but I enjoyed living with my in-laws because of the balance it offered. I appreciate though that this isn't the case for everyone. While it comes with many positives, for me, moving out also came with some challenges. We lived a pretty carefree life while residing at my in-laws' for a few months, moving into our own home brought with it real-life responsibilities—bills, mortgages, etc. Things got real. And with that comes stress and pressure but we created many beautiful memories in our new home from long strolls walking Bruno, our Rottweiler, to cosy nights in, to hosting gatherings of up to 40 people, BBQs and frequent fun games days. I've always loved hosting a memorable, hearty get-together! With time, we found our feet and settled well into the routine of living alone. It felt strange to be a proper grown-up!

Once we'd settled into our new lives, then came the "next stage"… Where I was a little jittery, Preetam was ready to become a father very early in our marriage.

I had a dream to visit my sanctuary, Sri Harmandir Sahib (The Golden Temple in India), before trying for children. Sri Harmandir Sahib has always been my sanctuary—I feel instantly warm and fuzzy when I enter my safe haven. I feel an instant spiritual presence and calm. I wanted to pray to God to hold my hand on this journey and to do whatever He felt was right for us. I wanted that comfort of knowing that something far greater than man was watching over me.

In September 2013, my wish was fulfilled. I remember that feeling of electricity running through my body the moment I set eyes on the beautiful Golden Temple during that visit. I felt relieved, I felt safe, I felt calm, I felt at home. It's a feeling I get every single time I visit. It's a feeling so difficult to articulate. It simply is my safe haven.

I remember Preetam and I walking in silence, side by side, as we inhaled the beauty and spiritual energy around us while deep in thought. "Arjun", I said out loud. "If we ever have a son, I'd love to call him Arjun."

"Harps, I was just thinking the same thing!" replied Preetam.

I came home with a feeling of a protective hand on my shoulder—God.

I felt slightly jet-lagged on our return but was due back to work the next day. I felt a little light-headed and the freshly baked goods for a colleague who was going on maternity leave literally made my tummy churn (definitely out of the ordinary for me—I'm usually the first one at the treat table!) but I thought nothing of it till I almost fainted a few days later at Sainsbury's. I decided to take a pregnancy test though I was pretty sure I wasn't pregnant already!

It was 4.30 am and we were both awake. I peed on the stick and walked back into our bedroom where I sat like an excited little girl. "Shall I go check?"

"Go!"

Preetam & I at Sri Harmandir Sahib in 2013

CHAPTER 3:

We're Pregnant!

TWO BRIGHT PINK LINES!

Lo and behold, we were pregnant!

I sat on the toilet and inspected the pee stick for what felt like several minutes in disbelief. Was I reading it right? Two pink lines meant pregnant, right?

Holy shit! I suddenly felt panicked. I hadn't expected we'd fall pregnant so soon. I thought I had a few months at least! Was I really ready for this?

Was I dreaming? It was so early in the morning and I felt delirious with tiredness and jet lag and, I guess, pregnancy hormones!

I quickly collected my thoughts as I remembered the struggles that some of our loved ones had faced on their conception journey and immediately was filled with gratitude.

I closed my eyes and took a deep breath and mentally took myself back to Sri Harmandir Sahib where I had prayed to God just a few weeks ago to bless us when and if the time was right for us—I took comfort in knowing that *this* was the right time.

Sheer joy washed over me. Everything in that moment felt like it had come together.

I scurried into our bedroom. It was dark and the light from our bedside lamp lit up Preetam's face. "WE'RE PREGNANT!"

"Oh my God, I knew it!" he squealed. He shot up and embraced me tight as he filled with emotion—his warmth felt so good. He was thrilled! He was made for this. Seeing his reaction made my heart swell and though I felt dubious at first, knowing how badly he wanted this, it gave me confidence that this was all happening just as it was meant. He was going to be the most incredible father and I knew I'd fall in love with him all over again.

And just like that, the concoction of the two of us began to grow inside me.

I've always found the notion of pregnancy incredible. It truly is a miracle how a human can grow inside a female and how they are solely dependent on their mother for nourishment, for protection, for warmth. I often find myself getting lost in thought pondering over so many of Mother Nature's mystical ways. Now, it was my turn to be that vessel to carry a brand-new human life!

The cynic in me *had* to take an additional three tests to quadruple check that I definitely was pregnant! We were only one-two weeks pregnant according to the Clearblue digital test but we were so excited to tell our immediate families. I spent the day making up personalised postcards on Microsoft Word featuring a cute baby cartoon and lilac background from *Baby B* for our parents and siblings. This baby was going to be the first grandchild for both sets of parents and I knew the news would bring everyone so much joy.

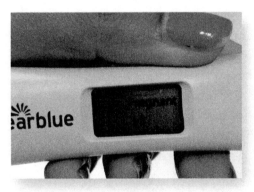

We're pregnant!

We were due to visit my in-laws that evening and I wanted to share the news with my parents on the same day so we popped by theirs beforehand. The journey felt so long; I just couldn't contain my excitement at sharing our news!

As we arrived at my parents' home, I had ants in my pants and before even asking how they were, I said, "This is for you, Nani (Nani being the term Grandmother from the girl's side)" and handed her the postcard. The penny didn't drop until she'd finished reading. "You're going to be a Nani and Nana Ji!" I spoke. "Oh my God!" shrieked my mum with her mouth wide open in surprise as tears began rolling down her sweet cheeks. My dad's eyes watered, filled with joy. His beaming smile behind teary eyes made me feel warm and fuzzy; he was an incredible father to us girls and I knew he'd be an even better Nana Ji to his grandchild. They'd get to experience his love, kindness and warmth and I couldn't wait!

My sisters were thrilled as they too were overcome with emotion at the thought of becoming masis—something they'd been waiting for too! I knew they were going to be the best aunties to *Baby B* and that he or she would be spoilt rotten!

We didn't hang around at my parents' as I wanted to go straight to my in-laws to share the news with them. I knew they would be ecstatic—they were made for this!

We got back in the car and headed straight there. Again, I felt that same adrenaline as we drove to Harrow. "Hurry up!" I groaned Preetam as we seemed to hit every red light en route. I just couldn't wait!

We walked in and handed over the postcards; my mother-in-law and father-in-law popped on their reading glasses and carefully scanned the postcard.

"You're pregnant!" said Mané who sussed it first.

They were all over the moon! My mother-in-law and father-in-law had been waiting for this since we got married. I remember my mother-in-law asking me the night before our wedding, "So, when are you going to make me a grandma?" behind a cheeky grin with a nudge, nudge, wink, wink—she was obviously referring to our legal obligation to consummate the marriage on our first night. Haha! They couldn't wait to be grandparents! Mané and Indy were also so excited—their first niece or nephew was on their way and I knew they were going to be so loved by their pua ji (auntie—dad's sister) and chacha ji (uncle—dad's brother).

I downloaded not one but multiple pregnancy apps as we eagerly followed our baby's growth journey and how he or she would evolve from a blueberry to a watermelon! I'd send screenshots of the baby's development each week in our WhatsApp family group chats as our family also lovingly followed the growth of their youngest member. I felt so grateful to have our family's shared love and excitement.

I'd sit on our bed with the winter sun beaming through our bedroom window as I lovingly took time to write to my unborn baby in my personalised pregnancy journal—taking care with how neat my handwriting was—I wanted everything to be perfect. I shared my hopes and dreams, my undying love and my sweet musings. I carefully kept all my scan pictures in that same journal.

I'd frequently visit the Gurdwara and ask for God to guide me and to keep us safe. I'd play kirtan to my unborn baby. It gave me a sense of security, love and safety.

During my first trimester, I had a few scares due to spotting but after a few scans, all appeared normal; thanks to the Almighty. It was a huge period of adjustment; getting used to the morning sickness (always whilst brushing my teeth), the constant feeling of tiredness, the loss of appetite, the constant worry for my unborn child and the reality that I was soon going to be a mummy! I found that sniffing lemon candles helped with the sickness, as did ginger biscuits!

As we approached 12 weeks, I combed the internet for cute pregnancy announcement ideas to share our news with the wider family—I wanted to channel my creativeness into an exciting announcement, especially as it coincided with Christmas! We have an annual gathering with Preetam's side of the family on Boxing Day—all his cousins, aunts and uncles, and it felt like a perfect time to share the news. The results of our nuchal screening following our 12-week scan aligned perfectly with Boxing Day. I decided on personalised Christmas crackers that I made which included a candy dummy and a baby scan picture. I had all the time in the world to hand-make our announcement idea as I poured my heart and soul into the excitement for our unborn baby.

Boxing Day arrived and I remember the butterflies in my tummy as we drove to Newbury to Preetam's cousin's house. After we'd feasted on our pot luck lunch, which merged into dinner as we overindulged, I asked everyone to sit in a circle to pull a cracker.

"Ready, steady, go!"

Crack!

It took about 60 seconds for the first person to realise what the cryptic baby-related items were for. We were welcomed with lots of excitement and warm hugs—*Baby B* was also going to be the first grandchild on this side of the wider family.

Our friends and remaining family were sent a picture of Bruno announcing that he was about to become a big brother. In hindsight, that did take a bit of explaining to be fair! The number of people who thought that Bruno was about to become a father was baffling!

We attended ante-natal classes run by the NCT (National Childbirth Trust). The different sets of parents were all on very different journeys and were from different walks of life, but we all had one thing in common—we were about to become parents for the first time! It felt nice to share that excitement with people who were going through it at the same time. We felt comfortable with them very quickly. Preetam certainly did—during the class where we discussed how our partners could help us during labour, the course tutor asked, "What would you do if your pregnant partner needed help turning over?" Preetam, being the gentleman that he is, answered, "Use a forklift!" The ice was truly broken after that!

I had this perfect vision of me in labour (I didn't watch One Born Every Minute to know any different!) with my hair and make-up intact; that was going to be me! Shallow, I know. I remember walking into one of our NCT sessions and seeing the walls plastered with real-life images of women in labour and had a mini shock! It's funny because most first time pregnant women I speak to feel that they'll have control of their labour when it happens. In reality, you can't really prepare for a) something you've not been through before and b) something that's steered by Mother Nature.

I wasn't someone who feared labour—I was actually excited for it!

I was so consumed in my baby bubble as my bump swelled with my tiny little human. I had the time to dream it all out—the routine, the breastfeeding, the labour, the skin-to-skin… it was going to be exactly how they show it in the glossy magazines. That would be me—immaculate during labour. I'd have this motherhood thing nailed. I was an organised person by nature, so why wouldn't I nail it?! I had zero shadow of a doubt.

Preetam and I would spend significant amounts of time pondering about what our life was going to be like. Who would our baby look like? Would it have the best of both or would the poor kid be doomed with my forehead and Preetam's nose?!

I spent hours browsing Pinterest looking for the most perfect nursery ideas; a cute safari theme is what we went for. I wanted every detail to be immaculate and even ordered my desired decals and matching bedding from America. We took our time to lovingly decorate our baby's room; it made everything feel so real.

I enjoyed purchasing maternity clothes to dress my beautiful blossoming bump. I was spoilt by both sets of parents with my favourite food and being forbidden to do any housework while in their houses! I was so careful with what I ate, ensuring I didn't consume any non-pasteurised ingredients and limiting my caffeine intake. Preetam would lovingly be at my beck and call for any cravings—my regular being slush puppies, chilli and lemon crisps, paneer and vegetable samosas. I couldn't stand the smell of cooked eggs or stir-fry!

I was enjoying every single part of the build-up to our baby arriving—from decorating the nursery, to filling the wardrobes with cute outfits, to eating whatever my heart (oops, I mean my baby) desired, to packing and repacking my hospital bag multiple times! But there were moments of fear which crept up every so often.

After my first trimester, I started making a shopping list for the baby. I felt so apprehensive about even putting a list together—I felt like I was tempting fate. We took our time carefully researching strollers and car seats and our home slowly filled with the essentials as my belly grew. Though I was excited, my anxiety was through the roof due to my existing diagnosis of hypertension. I had more scans than I can even remember. We spent an absolute fortune on private scans. I needed constant reassurance that everything was okay. It kept me sane. It was my way of having some form of control; just knowing all was okay. It was my first pregnancy and I had a constant fear of something "going wrong". So much so that we even had our nuchal and anomaly tests repeated at Harley Street. It was reassuring having lengthy scans, admiring the beauty of nature and how a whole entire human was growing inside me; something that I still can't get my head around. I always kept myself grounded in knowing that not every pregnant woman was able to do this—it was a privilege to be able to afford private scans to ease my anxiety.

From the beginning of my pregnancy, I was under consultant-led care as I was at high risk of developing pre-eclampsia due to my hypertension. Pre-eclampsia is a condition that some women develop during their pregnancy whereby the consequences can be fatal if undetected and unmanaged. By my second trimester, I

Baby B bump

was going to day care twice a week to be monitored; the appointments lasted on average two hours each time but sometimes as much as four. Though it became tiring, I took comfort in knowing I was being monitored closely. I really got to know all of the midwives on the maternity ward. They provided me with so much care, comfort and reassurance. Getting to know them would serve me well during labour!

I was also seeing my consultant, Mrs G, at least once a month by this point and had a really great rapport with her. She was brilliant at discussing things with us and was so attentive to understanding my mental health needs as well as my physical, as opposed to simply calling all the shots. She was an absolute Godsend and I felt blessed to have all the right people surrounding me through this precious journey.

I was 25 weeks pregnant and we were getting ready to catch our flight to Dubai that evening for our last baby-free holiday with my family. We were about half an hour away from leaving for the airport when I felt a little swish. "Oh my God, Preetam! I just felt a kick!" He jumped up in glee. I squealed with delight as Preetam rushed over to feel. It felt bizarre! There was an actual limb prodding! We stole a moment before leaving for our flight and both lay on our bed for a few moments with a hand each resting on my belly basking in amazement. This became a frequent scene as the days and weeks passed; the amazement never wore thin. With the kicks came great comfort in knowing the baby was okay.

I felt nervous going to Dubai. The thought of being thousands of miles away from home and something going wrong dawned on me. Mrs G jokingly offered to come with me; little did she know I'd have packed her in my suitcase if it was an option! She told me to go and enjoy my holiday and that the baby would be none the wiser in which country I was currently in and so I did just that.

I ate all the food my growing belly desired as I couldn't distinguish between a craving and my own mind! I enjoyed the relaxation as I rested my now-swollen feet and loved having the time to run away with my thoughts as I had the comfort of my baby's kicks letting me know that all was okay. I embraced being away with my family. I reminded myself that this was our last holiday without a child. What would our future holidays look like? Would we still travel? Holidays would certainly be different—"You'll be spending the time running around after a child rather than sipping on mocktails whilst leisurely lazing on a sun lounger!"

When we returned, it was time to plan for labour.

We made the decision, together with Mrs G, for me to be induced at 39 weeks as my blood pressure was creeping up. We took time and care in my birth plan. Ultimately though, she reminded me that they would make decisions based on the safety of both the baby and me and to trust them. I kept my birth plan very loose as I knew there were so many options—forceps, ventouse, C-section—and I wanted to work with the professionals in deciding the best course of action for me when the time came. I did have a list of desires for when my baby was born though, whatever method it was born by. My list looked something like this:

- Skin-to-skin as soon as *Baby B* is born
- Make sure paat (prayers) is playing
- Preetam to cut the cord
- Place kara (silver Sikh bangle) on baby's wrist

Even though I was prepared for deviation from the plan, this list was very important to me.

Though I spent my days centred on our unborn baby and our future, a growing belly, and frequent kicks and punches, it still felt surreal.

My third trimester got harder as I got bigger and developed sciatica and carpal tunnel but wrist splints fitted by the hospital really helped with the latter. I was hospitalised a few times due to fluctuations in my blood pressure and increased risk of pre-eclampsia and palpitations. It was nerve-wracking but I had the constant reassurance of my little baby's punches, kicks and rolls to know all was okay. Being hospitalised was odd as I was surrounded by other women at different stages of pregnancy. Some were in the early stages of labour, some looked so composed, whilst others were bawling; some were admitted for the same reason as me whilst others were still very early on. I wondered how I'd cope when in labour.

I was wishing my time away. It was a rollercoaster of anxiety and excitement and I just wanted baby to be here safe. Yet, as I got closer to the finish line, I almost wanted to hit the pause button as I realised how much my life was about to change. I decided to go on maternity leave seven weeks prior to baby arriving so I could truly absorb and enjoy the build-up. I spent days lying on the sofa with a blanket, binge-watching a Netflix series, going for spa dates with my sisters, going for lunch dates with my parents, afternoon teas with my friends and shopping trips with Mané and just making the most of my alone time. I fully made the most out of my seven weeks off and really enjoyed that time. As much as I was excited to have a little human as a sidekick, I was quite nervous at the thought of having my life centred around someone else; as selfish as it sounds. I was used to being able to do my own thing without any limitations—that was about to change.

I was spoilt rotten with a beautiful jungle-themed baby shower organised by my sisters, Mané and Amrit, where we played games, ate lots and pondered over what *Baby B* would be like! It was a beautiful sunny day— the perfect setting for what was to come. I was full of gratitude for being surrounded by my family and friends. I felt overwhelmed by the amount of love that was present in the room—they were all there for *Baby B*. My crazy aunts, who never fail to provide the most entertainment and make our generation look super-boring, made sure it was a day to remember with their group re-enactment of labour based on their own experiences! Haha! It was in the moments after the shower as our guests started leaving that the reality started setting in and Preetam and I were left standing amongst piles of baby items.

I was about to become a mummy!

CHAPTER 4:

All Systems Go!

GOING IN FOR AN INDUCTION as excited as I do when we go on holiday! We'd chosen a Sunday with the hope that I'd be in established labour by the Monday when Mrs G would be on duty. That was my control freak side doing the thinking for me but of course the reality is, where Mother Nature is concerned, we have little to no control!

We arrived at the hospital at about 3 pm.

I was told they'd start by inserting a pessary—fun! If you've ever had a smear test (I hope you have if you're due!), if you're anything like me, the moment that dildo-type thing comes anywhere near me, I cease up—not the easiest way for it to slide in! The same was true of the pessary. My body tensed up as the gentle midwife tried to insert it; it didn't hurt, it just felt uncomfortable. I was relieved once it was in!

I settled in and got comfy. It was like something out of a comic sketch, to be honest. I set up all my things like I was on vacation; I made full use of the bedside cabinet and my little table. As I settled on the bed, within a few minutes, I was abruptly interrupted—my contractions came on fast and heavy. Within an hour or two, my contractions were every three minutes. I had told Preetam to go back home to let Bruno out and Goov had arrived. I showed her how solid my bump was every time I contracted—"Wow! The human body does that all by itself? Insane!"

"Take my phone and log it!" I said to her, referring to my contractions and an app I was using to monitor them.

She had kindly made me pasta bake and garlic bread but I didn't feel like eating and before I could even open the lid, the midwife came in to check me. "It's time to go down to the labour suite! The baby is on its way!"

"WHAT?!" I'm not sure why I was so surprised, but it wasn't part of the plan I had conjured up. Preetam still wasn't back and I was rushed down to the labour suite with my terrified sister, Goov, who had not planned to be with me during labour. She gathered my belongings (I don't travel lightly and I'd packed as though I was going on a vacation for a week!) as I was wheeled down to the labour ward.

Though taken by surprise, I was so excited as the adrenaline kicked in. "The pain will be over before you know it and you'll have your little darling in your arms!" I thought. Goov called Preetam who arrived in four minutes and met us just as we entered the labour ward.

Everything seemed to be moving super-fast.

The senior midwife came in. She set me up to monitor my contractions. It felt very warm, these contractions coupled with the scorching heat in the middle of a very hot summer. I scanned the room between contractions—phew, the Dyson fan.

"Regular strong contractions, I think this baby will be here tonight!" she said eagerly. The excitement of meeting our little human made for a great distraction during contractions. It was the kind of excitement that makes you want to grit your teeth and jump for joy.

It was all coming together so pleasantly! This wasn't as bad as some of the horror stories I'd heard!

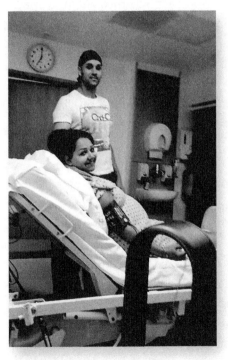

In labour ward when we thought
Baby B was on their way!

After faffing for what seemed like ages, the midwife checked how far dilated I was.

I shrilled as the midwife swept deep inside me sending a shooting pain through me. Preetam held onto me as I sobbed in pain. Goov stood looking stunned.

"Oh", said the midwife.

"What's the matter?" I asked. I was 0 cm dilated and in so much pain. I felt deflated.

The pessary had induced contractions but hadn't caused any dilation. There was going to be no baby any time soon. Goov had resumed the role of messenger and was keeping our families up to date. She soon toned down their excitement as she shared that it wasn't about to happen just yet.

I was given pethidine (which I'd sworn against!) and sent back up to the ward. I really didn't want to take pethidine because we'd been taught in NCT classes that it passes through to the baby and can make them very sleepy. It felt like such an anti-climax. I was so tired that I didn't even get to eat the pasta and garlic bread, something I'm still sad about today!

I fell sound asleep and Goov snuck out to get some rest.

After all the adrenaline and excitement (and pain), there was nothing. I'd hoped that my regular contractions meant that my baby was going to be with us soon. I decided to make the most of whatever time I had at the hospital—with the hustle and bustle of everyday life, it wasn't often I got time to just sit back and do nothing (apart from contract!). I suspected the baby would be here within a day or two.

That night, I had broken sleep between contractions but was hopeful. Having witnessed the winning tag team that Goov and Preetam had been the night before, I decided to ask Goov to be my second birthing partner. It was something I knew she'd be really uncomfortable with but something I really needed. She reluctantly agreed. She spent the day with me, helping me walk around and letting gravity do its job, running up and down and taking turns with Preetam to get me my favourites—Costa Peach Lemonade and cheese and tomato paninis, while also sending updates to the family. She slept the night at our house to help Preetam manage Bruno while also spending time with me.

48 hours later. Still no dilation. Everyone would go to sleep with their phones on full volume waiting for the call that just wasn't coming. How much longer was this going to last?!

68 hours later, a pessary, two lots of gel and six internal examinations later… I was *still* 0 cm dilated. This meant it was almost impossible for them to break my waters with no way in.

By now, I was exhausted and done with the positive self-talk and trying to psyche myself up. The excitement had been replaced with frustration, disappointment and tiredness. My contractions were still intense and frequent and my TENS machine was my best friend.

I was really grateful to be given my own room for the duration of my stay and was also allowed to have one visitor during non-visiting hours which helped the time pass. I was allowed to have someone stay overnight but the midwives did such a great job of ensuring I was as comfortable as I could be in riding through the contractions that on a couple of the nights, I encouraged Preetam to go home to get some rest to prepare for life after labour!

Claire, a midwife who we'd had a brilliant rapport with from the first meeting suggested I opted for a planned C-section. I remember her vividly explaining to me that it would be a lot more sensible to go down that route than to try and force my waters to break as there was no certainty that the IV drip would work and I may end up needing an emergency section instead. But I was adamant in wanting a natural labour, especially as I'd endured days of pain already. I had forgotten to "go with the flow" as originally discussed with Mrs G a few weeks earlier.

The consultant on duty decided that if I didn't go into established labour during the night, I'd be taken down to the labour ward the next morning where they'd attempt to break my waters. I was kept nil by mouth from then on. It was now day four.

I managed to get a little sleep that night and woke up half a centimetre dilated. "Yes!!"—I was excited as it meant I had more of a chance of them successfully breaking my waters.

I woke up with butterflies in my tummy (not sure if it was hunger or the excitement!). I put on light make-up before going down (crazy, I know)—I hadn't forgotten that immaculate image I had of myself during labour, and although it hadn't started off great, I knew I was near the end!

I was taken down to the labour ward first thing where they would administer an epidural and force my waters open! They weren't sure whether they would be able to break my waters as my cervix was too far back and I wasn't dilated enough. Great.

I prayed and prayed. I had come so far and yearned to have a natural birth. I *wanted* to experience it.

Before they could administer the Pitocin IV, I needed an epidural. Panic. "You've got this", I told myself.

The registrar came in; she looked friendly and I felt a little calmer. I took a deep breath to slow myself down.

Preetam stood opposite me and embraced me in his arms as she prepared to insert the needle.

How big is it?

HOLY SHIT. Perhaps I shouldn't have looked.

"I'm about to insert", she said. I clenched onto Preetam for dear life anticipating how it would feel. I shrieked in pain as a pang travelled up my spine! *Nothing* could have prepared me for the excruciating pain.

"I'm so sorry, it didn't go in correctly." she said, panicked. Goov took my hand and squeezed it.

"Let me try again." I held my breath and sat really still.

I let out a shrilling scream. "Please let me try one more time." Please God, let this be third time lucky.

Preetam looked at me, helpless. He held me tight as I sobbed—an ugly uncontrollable sob. Why did this feel so difficult?

"Harps, remember that time when you…" Goov began recalling private sister jokes to distract me.

"OUCHHH!!!!" I screamed.

"Enough! Please bring someone else in!" Preetam exclaimed, no longer able to tolerate my pain and visibly feeling helpless.

A moment later, a senior consultant arrived. "I'm so sorry", he said as he applied a numbing spray to my back. I wasn't expecting that to be so painful either. Maybe it was because of the failed epidural attempts.

Four attempts and lots of tears later, the consultant finally managed to administer the epidural first time. I felt relieved as I let my body sink into the bed.

Now for the next challenge. "You're over the worst of it, Harps. You've got this."

Mrs L, a lovely female consultant arrived. She examined me. I was so sore below from having so many internal examinations over the past few days but I knew this would be one of my last.

"You're still only half a centimetre dilated and your cervix is quite far back but I will give it a go." she said. Stay positive, Harps.

She approached me with what looked like a captain's hook. Yikes! That has got to hurt, I was thinking.

It felt different to the pessary being inserted—maybe because I was so numb below and my muscles were relaxed. It also allowed her to travel further back and though it was uncomfortable, it wasn't as painful as it probably would've been without the epidural.

After a good few minutes, I felt a gush of water below.

"THANK YOU SO MUCH!" I shrieked with happiness. I was absolutely ecstatic! I was going to be able to deliver my precious little baby naturally!

Once I was comfortable (if that's what you want to call it—I couldn't move my legs myself), they administered "the drip" to artificially bring on established labour. I'd heard this part would be easy—that I'd be able to sleep till I was fully dilated as it would be pain-free, and it was.

Preetam and Goov settled themselves into their reclining chairs, positioned comfortably under the air-con unit—very welcomed given the humidity of the labour suite and a very warm June! I settled in my bed as we watched one of my favourite shows—The Real Housewives of Atlanta. I felt happy and content.

Moments later, the midwife slipped out and returned with a doctor who began scanning the baby's heart trace. "Please could you turn over?"

"What's wrong?" I asked, alarmed by her presence.

"The baby is sleepy and the heart rate is dropping. Please try lying on the other side so we can see if it wakes them." Suddenly, my tiredness disappeared as my fight or flight instinct kicked in.

I panicked. One of my beautiful NCT friends, Sup, had sadly given birth to her beautiful boy, Devraj, sleeping. She was texting me during labour—I'm not sure where she found her strength but her kindness is forever etched in my heart. She even offered to come and be with me despite the heart-breaking memories that same labour ward held for her.

The next 16 hours were spent with my midwife asking me to change positions every 15/20 minutes as my baby's heart rate kept dropping. I was exhausted from the past four days and I was so worried that something was wrong. I hadn't eaten a thing for what seemed like a lifetime and I felt weak. Still, I was grateful to the midwife for ensuring my baby was okay.

Suddenly, I felt the urge to push—

"I need the toilet!" I pleaded with the midwife as I feared I was going to shit myself!

"You don't need to go, I promise you! The baby is on its way!"

"I definitely need to go!" Such an odd sensation and though it's all part and parcel of labour, I was so worried at how embarrassed I'd be if I did poop myself!

The midwife reminded me that there really was no option to go to the bathroom given that I was paralysed from the waist down. I was physically, mentally and emotionally exhausted by this point and I felt weak having not eaten for over 24 hours so didn't put up too much of a fight!

I was told when to push due to the numbness—I gave it my best shot with my sister and husband egging me on.

"Come on, Harps, push!!"

"FOR FUCK'S SAKE, I'M TRYING!" I screamed back in frustration.

I continued trying to push for two hours, falling asleep in between contractions and being prompted to push by the midwife when it was time. I couldn't feel much and I felt so out of it.

Moments later, after doing a check down below, the consultant informed me that the baby's head was too far back and that I wouldn't be able to deliver naturally. They needed to get the baby out NOW as the baby's heart rate was compromised. Claire's words suddenly rang in my ears; she was right. I should've opted for a planned C-section. I was absolutely zonked.

Goov quickly gathered our belongings as Preetam slipped into scrubs.

Everything thereafter happened so fast. I was rushed to theatre for an emergency C-section, surrounded by about nine different people in scrubs as I zoned in and out. After about 60 seconds of pulling and tugging, "Congratulations, Mrs Bassan, it's a boy!" Our perfect little baby boy was born at 5.30 am on Thursday 26th June 2014 weighing seven pounds and eight ounces.

Arjun Singh.

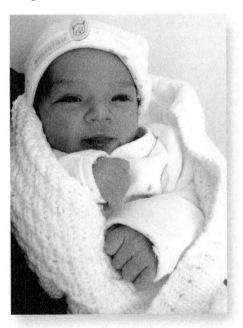

Our beautiful baby boy, Arjun Singh

Preetam passed Arjun over to me. I whispered, "I don't feel good" and handed him back. As he frantically got the attention of the people around us, I began to vomit and zoned out...

BLANK.

CHAPTER 5:

Feeling the Unexpected

FIVE HOURS LATER.
I woke up feeling dazed with the faint sound of
bleeping medical machines in the background. Where was
I? As I slowly opened my eyes, I realised I'd given birth.
I scanned the room through my blurred vision slightly
confused—I didn't have my contact lenses in and I wasn't
able to move to find my glasses. I caught Preetam lovingly
gazing down at Arjun in his cot. He was besotted. He had
dreamt of this moment. He was oblivious to me waking.
I remained silent as I observed them for a few moments.
I felt a pang of guilt and my eyes welled up.

I hadn't even held my beautiful baby yet. Did he even
know who I was? That I was his mummy? That he lived
inside me for nine months? We hadn't had skin to skin
contact as soon as he entered this world. Would he ever
love me? Did he have the best start in life and would he

be blessed without us having said our prayer that we'd planned? Was he scared when he was born without the comfort of me? His first feed wasn't my milk. Had I set him up for poor health? How did I let all this happen? Why the hell couldn't I just have pushed a bit harder? I felt like a failure and I felt so disappointed in myself. I felt like it was my fault and that my body and mind had failed me. My feelings were heightened by my physical paralysis from the epidural; my entire body felt like lead.

"Harps!" Preetam exclaimed as he spotted me, tears quickly streaming down his face. "How are you?" he asked as he hugged me and sobbed. "Where am I?" I asked him, confused. "In ICU; we've been in here for the last five hours… it was so scary, Harps" he replied.

Preetam was so tearful but so confident and so in love. He had thought he was going to lose Arjun and I. After I passed out, my heart rate and blood pressure had dropped and the medics rushed in to tend to me while prising Arjun off Preetam as his temperature fell. He was terrified—he had no control and feared the worst. He cried at the sight of his son and he cried at the sight of me as the thought of losing either of us was too much to bear. I didn't think it was possible to love Preetam more than I already did, but I was seeing a completely different side to him—one which made me love him even deeper than before.

"Would you like to hold Arjun?" he asked. "Okay," I said. Preetam placed Arjun on my chest. I felt blank. I felt a wave of doubt. We took our first family selfie where the confusion in my eyes was so visible. I placed Arjun

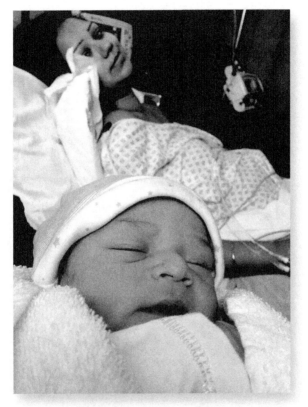

Shortly after I'd woken

on my chest and he began rooting for my breast. I felt comfort in knowing that that was something that only I could do for him. He latched on and I scanned this little human being that we had created and that my body had housed. I noticed that Preetam had placed his kara on him but we hadn't recited paat. I hadn't managed to accomplish much of my wish list for when he was born. I felt heartbroken.

Our first family selfie

These thoughts were soon interrupted by a sharp pain in my abdomen—the painkillers had started to wear off and I had to pause the feed. Then reality hit; Preetam had already fed him his first feed, changed his first nappy and had his first cuddle. All without me. Although I was so grateful to have Preetam there (he was absolutely amazing and so hands-on despite everything he had to witness), I felt so gutted. I was confused. I thought I was supposed to feel like I was on cloud nine after giving birth. That's what the magazines had shown. Why wasn't I feeling it? Why didn't I feel an instant connection? "It's because you didn't do skin-to-skin", I thought…

In reality, I wouldn't have been able to give birth naturally to Arjun as his head was too far up, but my rational side had done a runner. I should really have been focusing on the fact that my baby had been born healthy and alive. Yet, for some reason, my mind kept dragging me into a deep hole of self-hate; It was grim. It made me feel mentally more exhausted than I already was and I felt extremely selfish. I just wanted the best for my beautiful little boy.

The midwife brought me over some toast and jam with tea—jam on toast has never tasted so good, especially as it had been almost 40 hours since I'd last eaten! I felt like I had a little more energy.

I messaged my family and was pleased that they were all so overjoyed and thrilled. My mum was relieved that I was okay—only something I can appreciate as a mother myself now. This wasn't just about me; this was about our parents becoming grandparents—something they had waited for. They were so emotional and it made me forget about all my pain for a short while. I was so happy we were able to give them that gift. I couldn't wait for them to meet him.

I particularly remember my late Nana Ji (grandfather) and Nani Ji's (grandmother) reaction to the news that my mum had had a grandson; sheer joy. In the South Asian community, sadly, there is sometimes still preferential treatment for birthing a baby boy over a girl. My mum finally had a grandson to fill the void of her family's wish for her for a longed-for son. I didn't agree with the backward mentality, and I knew my mum didn't really either. There was sheer joy amongst my masis on the news that my mum had a grandson. Though the intergenerational beliefs that have filtered through frustrate me, I couldn't help but forgive them for not knowing any better. After all, they were five sisters and one brother. They'd heard the same sentiments their whole lives and where we are now so much more aware of gender bias, with a willingness to challenge gender stereotypes within our culture, that concept is still quite foreign to them.

Preetam had been awake for well over 48 hours—I suggested he go home to get some rest. Goov was on her way to the hospital to relieve him. When she arrived, she was so emotional at the sight of her little nephew and also overwhelmed with relief at seeing me. She's never been a "baby person" but she held him with so much confidence—like he was her own. I asked her to watch over Arjun whilst I slept. I was so tired and exhausted that I could barely keep my eyes open. I knew how uncomfortable she was around babies but I felt she'd do a better job than I would at that point. I fell asleep.

I knew the next few hours whilst I slept would be really daunting for her; she was as clueless as I was. Instead of panicking (which she'd normally do!), she got on with things for my sake—she knew I needed her. I also needed Harv, a natural with kids as a nursery nurse, but she was at work. I felt better knowing I'd see her that evening.

Goov taking care of Arjun while I slept

I woke up and Goov had changed his nappy (with a little assistance!) and managed to put him to sleep. Even my sister had changed a nappy before I did and managed to comfort my baby. The thought of having to lift myself out of bed and then lean over to change his nappy was frightening—I didn't understand where I was meant to find the strength to do it. My body was aching, my abdomen was throbbing and I felt drained. Despite this, I persevered with breastfeeding. I guess it was my maternal instinct wanting to provide for my baby. Harv joined us shortly after she finished work—she was a natural with Arjun. I felt so grateful to have my sisters there to support us.

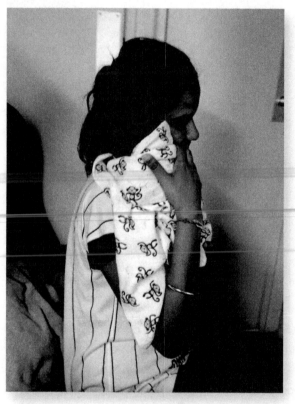

Harv with Arjun

I wanted my mum. I needed my mum. She always gave me strength. I knew she'd be at home praying for me.

Our parents and siblings came as soon as visiting hours started and the glee and emotion in our parents' eyes made me temporarily forget the agony I was in, both mentally and physically—it all felt so worth it seeing them.

"Are you okay, Harps?" asked my mum repeatedly as her focus was on me almost being able to read my soul through my overcast eyes.

"I'm okay, Mum, just in a little pain." I knew she felt helpless.

Our siblings came armed with gifts—I vividly remember Indy bringing a penguin costume for his new nephew. I plastered on a smile but behind it, my thoughts of self-doubt consumed the little energy that I did have. I could feel the love for Arjun—the grandparents were gloating with pride and Harv, Goov, Indy and Mané were bursting with excitement. Everyone was experiencing a new type of love. Preetam's mum's wishes from the day we got married had finally materialised. She was born to be an incredible Dadi!

As the family left, it was just Preetam and I. "This is us." I thought. My little family. I was grateful to have Preetam stay with me and to have our sisters stay at our house which wasn't too far from the hospital. Though I felt lost, I felt supported.

During the night, the midwives would come to have a cuddle and to help feed Arjun and put him to sleep; I learnt so many different ways of burping him and holding him! They were amazing and I still think of them today.

I looked forward to the nights where it felt less busy and where I had stolen moments with my angels.

We ended up staying for three nights after Arjun was born and then it was time to go home and begin our new journey.

CHAPTER 6:

Never Alone

ONCE WE WERE HOME AND settled, I was so used to being surrounded by at least Preetam and my sisters, that I steered clear of entertaining the idea of being alone; the mere thought sent me into a frenzy. I was terrified. I felt tired and physically weak—the exhaustion from labour was catching up with me.

I slowly became really reliant on Preetam and my sisters and began to lose any confidence that I could do this myself. I didn't change Arjun's nappy till he was two weeks old. TWO WEEKS!

My sisters were my constant. They went above and beyond anything I could ever have imagined. They both arranged for time off work so that they could be by our side to help both Preetam and I. They didn't even ask whether we wanted them; they were going to be there regardless. Whether it was changing nappies, the night shift, making lunch, helping me shower, doing the washing—the twins did it. I felt overwhelmed with gratitude but so underserving of their love and kind acts. I can be such a short-tempered so and so to them sometimes but they still bounce back and forgive me so easily. I constantly looked to them for reassurance. They say masis, are like second mothers *"Ma-jai si"* means "like a mother". Harv was a Godsend when it came to the night shifts. Sometimes Arjun would wake up seven to eight times and she'd be up before I'd even realised he was stirring. She emanates patience and has so much love for Arjun. Given he isn't their responsibility, they took on so much and I'm so grateful for that.

My constant supports—my sisters and Arjun's masis

Their presence alongside Preetam's made me feel so much more comfortable; I felt so useless. I wasn't mobile on my own—Preetam had to take me to the bathroom and help me shower so how was I meant to take care of my baby? I couldn't even place him down in his Moses' basket because it hurt so much. It just reinforced my self-opinion of being a failure.

I fell into a trap of self-destruction where I would constantly belittle myself. I had no idea how loud the voice in my own head was, so much so that I recognised it as others telling me the same. I said it to myself so often that I began to believe it.

Our parents and siblings frequently visited—Arjun was so loved. I'd be surrounded by a room full of people but still feel so lonely. How was that possible? I alienated myself—I felt like life was happening around me and I was a bystander. Nothing made any real sense. I felt so paralysed from my labour. I wasn't able to walk independently for a few weeks. I'd cry when Preetam showered me—how would he ever look at me as his wife again? My body was battered and I felt like an invalid. I felt ugly; how would he ever see me as desirable again?

Preetam decided to take an extra two weeks off from work (four weeks in total) to give me the emotional, mental and physical support that I needed. I was relieved.

Our first outing was to the Gurdwara to seek God's blessings and to thank the Almighty for giving us such a perfect little baby. I felt a lot more balanced in that moment—I always find that going to the Gurdwara centres me. I find it so peaceful. Though I usually loved

Mané and my in laws doting over the new addition

going to the Gurdwara, I was distracted by my pain. Moving was so difficult that everything took so much longer and I found it very tiring. I was no longer on morphine but on regular co-codamol and paracetamol and it wasn't doing much for me. I knew I had to keep trying to become better at being mobile because soon, Preetam would be returning to work.

As much as I loved breastfeeding, Arjun would sometimes be on my breast for up to 18-20 hours a day. I found it physically and mentally draining as I wasn't getting longer than an hour's sleep at any given time and it was taking its toll on me. Was this what my life was going to be now? I couldn't see past this stage.

Preetam made the decision for us that I would attempt breastfeeding during the day (my wish) and we'd bottle-feed at night so he could do the night shift and I could rest and recover. I was so thankful to him for calling that shot because had I made that decision, I probably would have beaten myself up over it. It really helped being able to sleep at night whilst he took care of Arjun. A mentally healthy and well-rested mum outweighed the benefit of me solely persevering with breastfeeding and it further fuelling my already-compromised mental health.

By three weeks, I'd given up breastfeeding as I was really struggling to cope with it—my little milk-guzzler was constantly hungry and I struggled with the excruciating pain I felt when Arjun's gums would break through the skin and cause bleeding. I also knew it would hinder me from going out comfortably and I'd end up spending even more time at home than I wanted to— my own mental battle. Giving up breastfeeding wasn't an easy decision either—something that I questioned myself on frequently—it was another "thing" I had failed him on. I questioned whether I was going to be able to form that same bond with him. I soon realised that even with bottle-feeding, your baby gazes into your eyes the same way. While I agree that breast is best, it just didn't work for me and I felt the pressure from the health visitors until I met one really lovely one who reassured me that the reason there can be such a push is due to low statistics in our area. Bottle-feeding also meant that Preetam could form a bond with Arjun too. I'd often do skin-to-skin with Arjun while bottle-feeding him.

Preetam was still on paternity leave. On about the third week, when it was just us, he said, "I'm off to the gym." I was so hurt, so angry that he'd leave me with Arjun alone knowing I didn't feel capable of taking care of him. As I heard the door close, I sobbed loudly. How could he be so selfish? How could the gym be his priority right now?

When he arrived at the gym, he texted me, telling me he'd left me on purpose because he had every faith in me and he wanted me to see that I could do it myself. I thank him for that moment now. In hindsight, he probably needed the break too.

During that time, I changed Arjun's nappy, let myself enjoy a cuddle with him and also spent a while gazing at our reflection in the mirror—I really had become a mother. That gorgeous face staring back at me was *our* son. How had he felt like such a stranger when he'd grown inside *me* for nine months?

The night before Preetam's return to work, I remember panicking. How was I going to do this? Was I going to be able to care for my baby all alone? Everyone told me I'd know what his cries meant—but I didn't! Did that mean I was a bad mum?

Preetam and Arjun had an indescribable bond—I always assumed it was to do with Preetam caring for him in the first few hours of his life, it was beautiful. I was grateful to have a hands-on partner, and watching them together made me love him even more. I always reasoned with myself that allowing Preetam to help feed Arjun via a bottle meant that they'd spent ages gazing into each other's eyes. That explained the way Arjun would look at him, his mannerism around him and vice versa. I felt really lucky to have a husband that was able to handle things how Preetam did.

How would I ever be able to match that for my son?

I wasn't able to drive; I could just about manage to move comfortably alone by this point. What if I fell down the stairs with Arjun? What if he didn't want to be with me because he had become so used to everyone else? What if he rejected me? I felt so down, so useless and so scared. Even the smallest task felt like a huge challenge and everything was starting to cave in on me. I felt stuck in my own head.

I couldn't bring myself to take Arjun to baby groups unless someone was with me and even then, these trips were few and far between. My negative thoughts would overwhelm me and my fear became greater than my desire to take him. What if he started crying? What if I didn't know what he wanted? What if I forgot something? I felt nervous. My confidence had disappeared. I didn't recognise myself anymore. I was experiencing such alien feelings from those I had expected to feel. I had no idea how to change them, or how to cope.

My health visitor, Heather, was coming to see us often and on what was meant to be her penultimate visit, she did a mental health questionnaire which I answered truthfully. The questionnaire revealed that I was presenting with many of the symptoms of Post-Natal Depression (PND)—something I'd heard of in passing.

I knew I was prone to depression. It was triggered after a road traffic accident I had in 2009. I was left with a fractured skull and suffered from post-traumatic stress disorder (PTSD). I was on holiday with my mum in India and we had just attended a kirtan programme in a town called Batala for the anniversary of the death of a family friend and I had done kirtan at the Gurdwara. It was about 5 pm and my mum suggested we perhaps go to Chandigarh the following day as it was getting late. Others echoed my mum's suggestion. I was adamant about going—I wanted to meet my cousin who was also there and my mum succumbed to my stubbornness.

I sat behind the taxi driver's seat and my mum sat next to me. I remember a Punjabi Bhangra track, "Heer", blaring through my headphones as I gazed out the window as we passed the raw roads and small shacks. We were driving at approximately 60 kph when our driver decided to overtake the car in front on the wrong side of the road—something that's quite common in India and usually dodged through the honk of a horn.

CRASH.

CHAPTER 7:

Flashback

THE CAR SPUN AROUND and I felt light-headed as my head smashed back and forth into the headrest pole in front of me (the driver had removed the headrest cushion). Suddenly, I felt myself floating into space oblivious to the injury that the impact had left on my head. I fell into my mother's lap as I further floated above the noisy and chaotic street and into white, soft, pillow-like clouds, my pain muted. My mother let out a scream from the pit of her belly as I lay in her arms with my head open, my flesh exposed. I was none the wiser. It was *that* scream that brought me back to reality and back into this world. I *had* to fight this for her.

I wasn't panicking; I was calm, quiet as I lay in my sobbing mother's arms. I could hear her trying frantically to call someone, anyone, as the taxi driver got out to argue with the other driver. My mum's desperation mounted as everyone's phones seemed to be off or unattainable.

Being a mother now, I can only imagine the sheer pain she would have felt with her child lying in her arms with their head split open in a foreign place with no one we knew in sight. There is no such thing as 999 in India.

I mentioned that I feel like my mother's prayers have always carried us through life and what happened next is one of the reasons why.

A world-renowned kirtani (priest who sings religious hymns), and also a close friend of the family, Bhai Niranjan Singh Ji happened to be passing along the road across from where we were. His backing vocalist said, "Wow, that looks like a really bad car accident." As they passed the road, Bhai Niranjan Singh Ji said they felt they heard our familiar voices. Of course, they didn't as if you've been to India, you'll know how chaotic and noisy the roads are with the honking horns and motorbikes and general hustle and bustle. When he glanced into the road as they approached the crossroads, he said, "Oh my goodness, they are our people."

Bhai Niranjan Singh Ji resides in India, but whenever they came on tour in the UK, for the last six years, they had stayed at our house. What were the chances that they'd be passing us in India at exactly that time? It was literally a few minutes after the accident.

Bhai Niranjan Singh Ji rushed us to a local village hospital. Upon arriving, they asked, "Has she vomited?" As soon as the door was opened to get me out, I vomited blood.

Panic.

The doctors panicked that I may have internal bleeding and was taken for a CT scan immediately. The doctor was astonished that I was alive let alone left without brain injury.

I was extremely drowsy—I was there, but not there.

I was rushed into theatre to be stitched up without anaesthetic—the most painful thing I can remember. Bhai Niranjan Singh Ji stayed with me, constantly reassuring me.

"Where is my mum?" I asked in my state of almost subconsciousness.

"She is okay", replied Bhai Niranjan Singh.

"Is she dead?" My adrenaline kicked in as my eyes welled up.

"She is okay", he replied.

After theatre, I was relieved to see that my mum was alive. She hadn't come with me as she also had to be checked. She was in complete shock. Everything had happened so fast.

"Mum, are you ok?" I said between sobs.

She was beside herself processing what had just happened while the fear of losing her child overwhelmed her. I glanced up at Bhai Niranjan Singh Ji. "You saved my life; thank you." He smiled behind frightened eyes and said, "It's okay, I nearly broke my back carrying you." He laughed trying to mask his shock. His face was as white as his kurta pyjama (Indian attire of a white long top and pants) had been prior to it being dyed with my blood. I truly believe God had sent him as his own messenger to save us.

I didn't know what I looked like. I stayed at the village hospital where I requested they cover all the mirrors as I couldn't bear to look at my disfigured face. The doctors were unsure about whether I'd lost vision in my left eye which was left so severely black and bruised, I was unable to open it. I didn't see my own face until four days after the collision and I was devastated.

My sisters and dad flew to India within a few days of the accident—their visas held them back from flying out immediately.

Though I felt really low, I was surrounded by family and friends who I felt so grateful for—people who went out of their way to look after us and ensure we had the best possible care; I chose to see the silver lining. I believed that my mum's prayers literally saved my life. Though I had no other injuries, the impact resided in my knees and I was unable to walk unaided. I had to have a bed bath. I was unable to go to the bathroom alone. I felt devastated that my mum had to take me to the bathroom to help me wash. It felt so wrong.

I was allowed to fly home six weeks later. On my return, I was told to go to the GP straight away. As soon as I arrived, I was told, "You need to go straight to A&E. We will tell them you are on your way and to see you straight away." I wasn't expecting that. I was very tired but I mentally felt strong by focusing on how much love and support I had. On arriving at A&E, I was rushed in and had a CT scan.

"Miss Virdi", said the maxillofacial doctor, "I'm really sorry to inform you, but we need to perform emergency

surgery—your fracture is healing towards your brain."
Just like that, my positive mental state shattered into a
million pieces and it set me off on a downward spiral. I
felt angry; deflated; gutted. My parents were devastated.
When would this end?

It was then that I truly learnt to appreciate my
beautiful family—their love and physical support meant
everything to me. I gave myself comfort in believing that
through this experience, my lifetime quota of dealing
with shit was done with. With the support of a counsellor
and cognitive behaviour therapy (CBT), I somehow got
through but it triggered separation anxiety which was
heightened by my mum's heart attack.

I truly believe my life was saved by a higher force, a
higher power—my Waheguru (God).

That's the very short version.

CHAPTER 8:

A Diagnosis

BECAUSE OF THE ROAD TRAFFIC accident and the impact that it had on my mental health, I was very aware of how prone I was to depression but *because* I was so aware, I thought I'd be able to control it. Have I mentioned I like to be in control?! Not quite the case when your body is raging with hormones and when the course of action is completely different to how you imagined it.

As honest as I was with answering the health visitor's questionnaire, I was so fearful of social services getting involved. Was my baby going to be taken away from me? Would I be classed as an unfit mother? What did this mean?

I described to Heather how everything felt so "big", overwhelming and challenging, and how I couldn't even bear the thought of leaving the house because it felt like such an ordeal.

"How about taking Arjun into the garden to eat lunch?" she asked. In her mind, it was probably a sensible suggestion given we are blessed with a beautiful garden space and it wasn't really going "out". I explained to her that the task seemed far too big for me—it wasn't just a case of sitting outside, it was packing the things I needed for the baby, putting out a mat, taking out some sort of shade, taking out my lunch, taking out his bottle, ensuring the dog was locked away, plus how was I meant to transport everything to the garden whilst leaving the baby inside? I conjured up a huge mental wall—each brick I laid was another reason for me *not* to do it.

My brain was processing things in a complicated and irrational manner. Even though I knew it was irrational, I couldn't help myself. There was a mental block which made me feel stuck—I felt like I was in quicksand and wanted to get out but physically couldn't. I'd catastrophize every situation and every time, I'd play out the worst outcome that could potentially happen. I found the simplest tasks so daunting and "long". I'd put myself off from doing things before I'd even tried. In the UK, PND impacts 10-15 percent of new mothers—a startling statistic—and I was one of those. PND doesn't only impact just mothers alone, it can also affect fathers and partners too.

Preetam supported me in the best way he could—mostly, by doing practical things and leading with parenthood when he could see I needed a break. I didn't openly speak to our parents about how I was feeling and assumed they'd not really understand especially given mothers had done this before and I couldn't imagine they'd have had the same struggles—it always felt like they were "built" differently. I often spoke to my sisters and Sav and Amrit about how I was feeling. They were my "safe" people to confide in. Mané was also great at understanding and recognising my struggles. One day, she took the day off to come and spend some time with us; she knew the emotions I was wrestling. She grabbed some lunch for us from M&S and helped me take Arjun's things into the garden for us to sit outside. Those kinds of gestures meant so much to me. People were taking the time to try and help by showing me it wasn't as big a deal as I'd made it in my head.

Enjoying the back garden with the help of Mané

The thought of taking him out for a walk was the same—packing his bag, taking the pushchair out, getting him dressed for outdoors. I'd often have thoughts of someone attacking us and him being kidnapped. Everything just felt like it was too much.

I also had this massive guilt that I was relying on others. Every day, my mum was lovingly cooking healthy home-cooked meals for me, followed by a spoonful of panjiri (a mix of nuts and superfoods considered to boost your recovery post-labour) lovingly prepared by my mother-in-law. I felt comforted by her presence but also guilty for allowing her to see me in the vulnerable state that I was in.

The thought of Preetam going to work and coming home and having to help me; the amount the twins had done; everything felt so overwhelming. I was overwhelmed by the support and continued to feel guilty for it. I almost felt undeserving.

Because I had been diagnosed with PND, Heather didn't discharge me right away. Instead, she continued to visit me weekly and we established baby milestones for me to accomplish, such as "Take Arjun for a 10-minute walk." We'd talk through the practical steps of being able to physically get out of the house because as simple as the goal seemed on the face of things, my brain would go into overdrive thinking of all the eventualities. Heather expressed that it may be a good idea for me to try counselling to work through my thoughts. I agreed. Despite this being a bit of a taboo within the South Asian community, I didn't see any shame in admitting my struggles and seeking help for them. In fact, I saw it as strength, especially because I now had the evidence from when I had the car accident that seeking support helped.

I was assigned a counsellor. My first session was on a super-hot day—it was a really warm summer in 2014. I rummaged through my wardrobe desperate to find something that would fit that wasn't frumpy maternity pants or plain Primark t-shirts that had sick stains on them. I felt a loss of identity—nothing fit, I didn't recognise my body anymore and my mind was filled with negativity. I settled for an oversized blouse, leggings and my Birkenstocks that had housed my swollen feet for the last two trimesters of my pregnancy. I put my hair up in my signature ponytail but couldn't be bothered to try make-up—it was far too hot and it felt like too much energy. I walked to the GP surgery feeling somewhat free. I didn't have the worry of taking a baby with me—Arjun was at home with Preetam.

Our street felt different, or was it the lens through which I was viewing it? I was a mum now. As I took each step closer to the GP's surgery, I wondered why I had not soaked these moments up before. Everything felt different—surreal almost.

As I entered the surgery, I let out a sigh of relief. I was here and this was the start of feeling better. I entered the room and immediately felt "off". I was greeted by a stocky gentleman. "Hi", he said, a little animated. "Hi", I replied.

"How can I help?" he asked. I felt a little baffled. Did he not know why I was there? Why *was* I there? I felt my palms get sweaty. My heart began racing. I felt sick.

The session was somewhat of a blur but I knew this wasn't the right person for me as I left feeling worse than when I had entered and it wasn't because of what we'd spoken about. I felt like he didn't take me seriously, like he didn't "get me". That "off" feeling I had as I'd entered was my intuition speaking—our rapport was off.

I came home feeling defeated. I cried as I tried to make sense of what had happened. Why was this man even allowed to meet with vulnerable women? Was he even trained to deal with post-natal mental health? I couldn't help but wonder how a woman in a more fragile state may have responded. I shuddered at the thought.

I spoke to Amrit and shared my experience as I fought back tears. What was I going to do? What was my exit? Amrit listened to me—she's always been great at that and she always offers sound advice. She'd make a pretty awesome counsellor, come to think of it! She suggested I contact the GP and explain the situation and request an alternative counsellor. I was reluctant. What if I was being offensive? It felt so out of my comfort zone but, at the same time, I knew I couldn't see him again and if I didn't turn up to an appointment, it would raise a red flag and that sent me into a panicked frenzy. I had to take action.

I nervously called the GP's surgery and explained the situation. They were incredibly kind and agreed to offer me a different counsellor. I requested a female—I just felt a female could understand my mind better in that moment.

Trusting my gut and listening to the advice of my best friend, despite it feeling uncomfortable, was the best thing I could have done for myself. The new counsellor was warmer and kinder and the rapport between us was great. She didn't ask patronising questions or minimise my feelings. She listened.

I continued to work through my fears and blockers with my counsellor and though some days, I really didn't feel like talking, I knew that skipping a session may raise red flags and so I persevered. The counsellor helped me rationalise my thoughts and I was released from their care only once my health visitor was comfortable that I was okay and that counselling was helping—that was when Arjun turned seven weeks old.

I found an easier way for me to get out a bit more was by doing things with friends; my NCT friends, my other friends with babies or my relatives with babies. It made a difference being in the company of others. Perhaps it was a comfort thing, knowing the mothers would know what to do if something happened. I still couldn't face being in public places alone with Arjun in fear of all the "what ifs".

My NCT friend, Fiona, would frequently reach out to check in. Being a little older than me and having 20 years' experience with kids through her nanny work, I took great comfort in her. To this day, she'll randomly send postcards to let me know she's thinking of me and that she's always there. Her thoughtfulness goes a long way.

I spent my days navigating through the minefield of emotions that I was facing. When Arjun was about four months, I'm not entirely sure what possessed me to, but I decided I'd quite like to start a blog for myself as an outlet and a form of therapy. I texted my sister Goov and asked her what she thought. My sisters and Preetam encouraged the idea and, with that, "Baby Brain Memoirs" was born. The name was suggested by Goov and it felt very apt. I typed to my heart's content as I dumped my feelings onto a word document. I reluctantly hit "publish". I was nervous to put my words out there but I wasn't expecting anyone to read it other than perhaps my mum!

I woke up the next morning and was taken by surprise at the number of messages I'd received from so many women who felt exactly the same. It was then I realised just how many South Asian women felt the same but didn't share for fear of feeling like they failed. And it was there that Baby Brain Memoirs began its journey. It quickly became my safe haven and a space in which I can open up.

I began writing my thoughts more frequently and sharing them—be it my fears, my wins, my good days, my bad days. I took comfort in knowing that I wasn't alone but it wasn't enough to stop me from feeling the heaviness. Much to my surprise, many warmed to my relatable content. The blog's purpose has become far greater than I ever intended as I began speaking up on subjects such as PND that was very much still considered a taboo within the South Asian community. I was fortunate enough that my parents encouraged me to speak openly and honestly—something that not all South Asian parents would be keen for their daughters to do!

CHAPTER 9:

Small Victories

WHILE I FELT A LITTLE INSECURE about Arjun's love for me, one thing that I always reminded myself of was that I knew him best and he knew me best—we'd known each other the longest. From the nine months that he lived inside me, his most familiar sound was my heartbeat. When doubt consumed me, I'd remind myself of that—that the most comforting sound and scent for Arjun would be me. Though we weren't able to do skin-to-skin contact immediately after birth, I'd often place him on my chest so I could feel his heartbeat and he could feel mine and I'd feel instant comfort.

Even a year on, I still had fears and I felt as if it hindered my ability to be a "good mum". I was scared to do things alone and sought comfort in having someone with me be it another mummy and baby or be it Preetam or my sisters. I didn't feel capable to do things alone; I didn't have the confidence.

I found many things which some would consider simple, really challenging—the thought of taking him to a shopping centre felt impossible and so far out of my reach. I set myself the goal of taking Arjun to Westfield shopping centre in White City (it *had* to be Westfield) ALONE one day—ambitious but I knew I'd feel amazing if I was able to accomplish it. The words "Westfield" and "alone" were enough to set my mind into overdrive and send me into a state of panic which eventually meant I would mentally shut down. This was a habit that had got worse since I became a mother—over thinking and talking myself out of things.

Seven months into my motherhood journey, I decided that it was time to face my fears.

The night before I had planned to go, I decided to pack Arjun's changing bag and take out his clothes as well as mine for the morning. That way when I woke up, I knew I wouldn't have that to add to my list of excuses of reasons to not go. I also ensured I didn't buy a few essential toiletries from elsewhere so I felt pressured into going as I desperately needed them for our forthcoming holiday to Dubai.

That night was exhausting. Arjun woke about five times so we both had very broken sleep. I woke up really tired but knew I had no choice but to go as I had to get the last few bits before we flew out. Had I not needed those toiletries, that trip never would have happened that day.

I fed Arjun, played with him for a little while, got ready, did my hair and makeup whilst he napped, got him ready and double checked all our bags. I consciously eliminated the time pressure I generally put on myself—I don't like being late anywhere, even on my own watch!

Arjun was calm, I was calm. I placed him in his car seat, strapped him up and did a double check of everything before we set off.

As I drove up, I had so many questions running through my mind; what if I lost something? Where was I supposed to put all our shopping bags? One of the items on my shopping list was a pair of Timberland boots for Preetam—how on earth was I meant to carry those with a push chair and a changing bag and manage a baby? What if Arjun kicked off? I could feel the self-doubt creeping in. I raised the volume of the car radio—Kisstory was playing some of my favourite old school tracks and I soaked up the gorgeous sun hitting my windscreen while trying to drown out the "noise" in my mind.

We reached Westfield 50 minutes later with Arjun stirring from his nap just as I parked up. He woke up pretty ratty which wasn't the best start to our trip. Again, I tried to remain calm. Amidst his screams, I remembered to note down where the car had been parked, to put the ticket in a safe place (the side pocket of my changing bag), to put my phone and keys in a safe place (in the pushchair pocket). I'm the type of person to lose the car ticket in the chaos and I was really conscious and slow paced because of it—I didn't want to end up in one of those situations!

I loaded Arjun into his buggy and we entered the building. Arjun calmed down at the sight of the hustle and bustle around us—all the new smells, the new faces and the bright lights were captivating to him. Meanwhile, I was busy trying to figure out what I was doing—I had completely forgotten that with a buggy, you can't take the escalator and I'd need to find an elevator instead. This was all new to me at and I felt flustered. I was greeted by smiling mums and their babies who were also on a similar journey to me. Very comforting.

Once the elevator door opened, it dawned on me that I hadn't really planned out my journey. It wasn't as easy as it was before—before I'd go to shops randomly and could quickly change my mind and rush back up to the next floor or down to the lower one if I had to. It wasn't that easy with a baby—I needed to systematically approach this so it didn't become laborious and I didn't have to keep locating lifts! It's funny how the simplest things in life change when you have a baby.

Once I'd figured out where we were going, we set off trawling through our list of shops. Arjun soaked in his new surroundings and I browsed the kids wear aisles at H&M. Arjun remained calm for the most part but halfway through H&M, he became frustrated and started fussing. It quickly escalated and he was inconsolable within minutes. I didn't know what to do—you always get mixed feedback from other mummies—some will say "Let him cry it's normal, babies cry." Some will say "Leave him in there otherwise he'll cry every time he wants to come out knowing you'll take him out." Others will say "Pick him up straight away—don't ignore his cries." I didn't know which voice to go with. I was so conscious of the other people around me. Were they getting irritated by his cries? Were they thinking I'm a bad mum for letting him cry for a few minutes? Did they think my baby was a "bad baby"?… Do I just walk out and leave the bits I'd picked for him? So much was running through my head at the same time. I had a hand full of clothes, a buggy to shift around plus a screaming baby.

I thought about it rationally—I was there now; I may as well just get on with it. I decided to let him cry whilst I quickly picked up his last few bits as I knew there was nothing "wrong" with him, he was just fed up of being in his buggy which was understandable. I knew though that if I took him out at this point, it would be mission impossible to get him back in. Carrying him plus manoeuvring the buggy around Westfield to the car park was going to be really tricky so wasn't really an option! We headed over to the queue to pay. There were a few people in front of me. Arjun was still crying. I got the odd glance but I ignored it—it may not have even been a negative glance. Once I had paid for our goods, I organised the shopping calmly. I tried to block out Arjun's screams whilst I did this. Once I'd organised things, I took him out for a cuddle. He was instantly soothed by my embrace and calmed down.

I put him back in his buggy after a few minutes. He started crying again but I didn't have much of a choice as we had to take the lift back down. We went to Timberland next as it was on our way to the car park and thankfully the shop was quiet. I bought Preetam's shoes and as Arjun had finally fallen asleep, I decided to head to another few shops before leaving. Bliss.

I browsed for some summer clothes for myself for our forthcoming holiday and just generally took the time to reflect on where I was at that moment...

I was alone.

In Westfield.

With Arjun...!

Arjun & I at Westfield!

I felt proud, overjoyed, empowered but also quite tired. What a milestone!

Though I had small victories, my days were still consumed by irrational thoughts continuously. Even before I had Arjun, I was pretty paranoid but becoming a mother heightened what was already there. My every action is meticulously planned based on my thought process which is derived from my fears and embedded inside me. Here are a few examples of the daily anxiety I was dealing with:

- Preetam would have to wait for me to put Arjun in the car and let me get in and lock the car doors every morning before closing the front door. I was so worried about a random person jumping out of nowhere and attacking us/kidnapping him.
- I was too scared to take Arjun alone to the park or for a walk because I was terrified that he'd get kidnapped.
- I was too scared to go into our garden when home alone with him as I feared someone would jump over the fence and attack us.
- Returning home from work was like a military operation for me to be able to hold my laptop bag, my handbag, Arjun's nursery bag, my house keys AND Arjun in one go to get in the house without having to go back to the car. Slamming the front door shut behind me once back was a relief and by then, my heart would literally be pounding especially if Preetam wasn't home before me.
- When Preetam would go to the gym in the evenings, instead of watching TV, the CCTV channel would

constantly be on in our house and I would be too afraid to even go to the toilet in case I missed anything.

- If my parents didn't answer my phone call, I'd fear something had happened to them.
- I'd often wake up in the middle of the night to check that Arjun was still breathing.

I know those of you with rational minds may think I'm a tad crazy based on some of the above, and even I knew it was irrational, but I couldn't shake it.

Chapter 10:

My Little Knight in Shining Armour

As Arjun reached around 10 months, slowly, he distracted me from my habitual way of thinking. He started calling me "Mama" and the power that his little voice uttering those words so lovingly had over me was unreal. It unearthed so many new emotions. It made me feel empowered, strong and fearless… okay, maybe not fearless, but it certainly made me want to puff out my chest, put on my big girl panties and deal with my anxiety and fears. If not for myself, then for him.

It's amazing; although he couldn't talk properly yet, and I don't really talk about my fears often in the house enough for him to have heard, he seemed to have some strange understanding of them. And it's exactly that—an understanding. He oozed patience (most of the time) and his mannerism when dealing with me was so different from how he dealt with Preetam. He was a lot gentler and more patient—he had no idea how much he helped me deal with things. How would he know? His pace had been perfect—just right without me tipping over the edge. His confidence was endearing and inspiring.

He loved being outdoors, and the guilt that possessed me by not being able to fully support him in his new adventures tore me to pieces. His support, coupled with my guilt, and my desire to want to be by his side in everything that he did and never wanting him to sense my fear and therefore, becoming full of fear himself, encouraged me to think less and face my fears of being outdoors alone with him.

He'd take my hand and clasp it tight, almost like he was reassuring me. *He* made *me* feel safe. How strange. Should I have felt guilty? I'm his mother; I'm his protector. It shouldn't be the other way around.

My little knight in shining armour

Once he learnt to walk at just over a year old, I began to take him for short walks. I'd still find myself looking over my shoulder and wouldn't dream of letting go of his hand but I felt a lot more confident having him by my side. We were able to enjoy the outdoors more and learn new words like "tree" and "sky". I still wouldn't take him to the park alone.

I felt more comfortable going into the garden alone with him—I wasn't always 100 percent comfortable, but he didn't give me the chance to overthink. He began to show me what it meant to just be in the moment—instead of fretting over an intruder, to just be in his little moment—that moment where that piece of grass he was showing me was the most fascinating thing.

It took me a little longer to stop obsessing over an intruder while Preetam was out but we did get there. We started to play with Play-Doh or do colouring without the TV on when daddy was out. And if it was on, it was filled with bright and bouncing images of *Baby TV* as opposed to the dreary colours of the CCTV. Bruno was always close by to ensure we were safe.

I never felt as comfortable as most mummies seemed, but for me, the minor progress I was making felt pretty major.

It took what felt like a lifetime to feel the confidence with Arjun that I'd always dreamt of, but it was about a year. I loved him so fiercely. He became my strength, my absolute everything.

I always wondered if we'd travel again after becoming parents as we both loved a good holiday. Arjun never held us back; instead, he joined our adventures! Holidays became even more meaningful after becoming parents and viewing the world through a child's lens. We travelled around the world from Dubai to Singapore to Santorini to Bali to Abu Dhabi. I was even spoilt with a family trip to the Maldives with my little unit for my 30th; it was pure bliss! Watching my 11-month-old sipping on coconut water straight out of a coconut, observing the baby sharks (back when there was a time you could say baby

Maldives for my 30th birthday

shark and it wouldn't be followed by "doo, doo, doo-doo, doo-doo"!) and trying new foods in pure paradise was magical. Things had felt like they were settling.

I mentioned earlier that I absolutely love party planning; I poured all my efforts and creativity into planning Arjun's first birthday. It was spectacular—from the jungle-transformed garden marquee to the live crêpe and hotdog stands, to the mobile farm we had there—it was an unforgettable party and I loved celebrating my baby's birthday. It was also a celebration for me of how far I'd come.

As I began preparing to return to work, Arjun also started his settling-in sessions at nursery. It was a whirlwind of emotions entrusting complete strangers to take care of your child—your most prized possession. We'd visited a few nurseries and had settled on our chosen one by following Arjun's lead—he seemed content and happy.

His first settling-in session felt strange. He went in bushy-tailed not knowing that we wouldn't be there with him. After dropping him off, Preetam and I sat in the car silently, not really knowing what to do with ourselves. Our lives had revolved so heavily around this little person that it was hard to know what to do without him there. What did we used to do before we had kids? His first session went really well and gave us confidence that he'd be okay.

I, on the other hand, was a little bit of a wreck.

I was going through a rollercoaster of emotions about Arjun starting nursery and the changes that were going to be happening over the next few weeks that followed (like all mums returning to work!). I had gone off on maternity leave knowing that my existing job wouldn't exist when I got back. It was a project-type role and I'd managed to close off all my projects prior to my temporary departure. Although change always makes me very anxious, I almost welcomed the change in this instance. It was going to push me to explore a new area of the business or area of accounting, although I knew it'd be a challenge—especially coming back after a whole year. A part of me hoped I'd at least go back to the same team so they knew what I was capable of.

While on maternity leave, I'd often doubt my capability as a mother. I'd only ever given Arjun a bath alone once. Yep. I wonder if such a mother even exists elsewhere?! How can it be that I was too scared to bathe him alone? To me, in my head, it felt like a *huge* task that I simply couldn't accomplish alone. What if he slips under the water? What if I drop him while taking him out?

It's strange that as I got closer to returning to work, my confidence as a mother increased. Although I still hadn't bathed him, my overall confidence as a mother had become far greater than my confidence as an employee, as an accountant and as a finance manager.

"Baby brain" is no myth—I'm a prime example of it. I didn't even remember what had happened yesterday, let alone how to do my job! I was feeling really nervous and scared about returning to work. Excel used to be my best friend, but even using it to put together bits for Arjun's first birthday party had proven a challenge! How on earth was I going to go back to macros, VLOOKUPs and advanced formulas?! I'm not the most confident person in general, but this had definitely been a huge knock to my confidence. I'm guessing I'm not the only mother who has felt this way after returning to work after maternity leave.

While I'd been off, I'd barely thought about work, but when I had, it was always very intense. I'd maintained regular contact with my old team/boss just as a constant reminder of the reality that I would be returning eventually.

On the few nights leading up to my return, I had been really restless. I was filled with panic and fear. Who will I be working for? What will I be doing? What will their expectation of me be? Will I even remember anything? How will I manage work and a baby? I felt like I was just about able to manage to be a half-decent mother, I just about managed to be a half-decent employee, and now, I was going to have to do both together as well as manage a whole house! The thought overwhelmed me.

A part of me also had glimpses of excitement when thinking about returning to work—it'd give me some "me" time, a chance to find myself as something other than just a mummy. It would give me more structure and routine. It would give me the chance to get dressed and feel good rather than spend half the day mooching in my pyjamas, though, I'd really miss doing that!

I was fortunate enough to be returning to work three days a week rather than full time. It meant I'd get to spend some time with Arjun on Thursdays and Fridays and catch up with our friends and family during that time.

I knew it was going to be a huge rollercoaster of emotions when it came to leaving Arjun at nursery. "I hope my baby is okay. I hope his key worker is patient with him. I hope he receives cuddles when he needs them. I hope he doesn't feel scared or alone. I hope he doesn't miss us to the point of despair. I hope someone helps him to fall asleep at nap time—is that something I've done wrong as a mum, not preparing him for falling asleep independently during the day? I hope he's excited to go. I hope he enjoys the food there."

Just thinking about those things would reduce me to tears—I was going to miss him so much. He had become my life. The thought of him crying at nursery and me not being there broke my heart. The thought of missing out on some of his firsts also saddened me. It hurt so badly but I knew I'd cherish the time we did have together so much more.

On his second settling-in session, he had cottoned on to the fact that we wouldn't be staying with him and was really upset. Naturally, so were we. When we picked him up, he literally jumped into my arms and burst out crying—it felt like he'd pent up his emotions while there but let them out as soon as he saw us. It really weighed heavy on me.

I remember one particular night before I went back to work. After an episode (or 10) of Mickey Mouse, I switched the TV off. He lay on the bed and I lay opposite him and he stared lovingly into my eyes as we listened to Simran (religious hymns). He didn't do that often. He'd usually be too busy bouncing off the walls. Every so often, his tiny lips would break into a smile and his eyes would light up. He didn't break eye contact with me at all until he fell asleep. In precious moments like these, I couldn't help but cry. When he saw my tears, he got up and put his arms around me. I wonder if he knew I was sad or if it was pure coincidence. Through my smile back at him, I was hurting. "He's so perfect. I love him so much." The thought of not being with him always hurt. The thought of us already being at the next stage hurt. The reminder that a year had flashed by and I felt like I didn't remember much of it also hurt. I always make everything so dramatic in my own head and it really frustrates me about myself.

When I started maternity leave, I had that constant reminder of "make the most of it because time flies"… I had no idea just how quick. I had no idea that I'd feel this way. Even halfway through, I used to say, "I'll be okay when I return to work. It'll do Arjun and I both some good." and although I believed there was some truth in that, it still hurt. The nursery staff told me he was a happy boy and spent much of his time playing and crawling around. I felt so incredibly sad inside as I mulled over the change. This change that I was facing was no surprise and nor was it any different to the changes that most mothers and families face.

The night before I was due to return to work, we had a rough sleep. I felt a combination of fear, dread and heartache. I was filled with emotion. I lay there beside Arjun watching his peaceful face as he slept for the last hour. My heart felt like it was overflowing with love and my throat was struggling to fight back the tears.

At 2 am, I heard the sound of Arjun stirring. I nudged Preetam to get him to tend to him as we'd agreed that he'd do the night shift Mondays and Tuesdays and me the rest of the week. Instead of going straight to Arjun, who would have still had his eyes closed at this point, he decided to go to the bathroom first. Men! While he was in the bathroom, Arjun ended up in a fit of tears while waiting and woke himself up fully. Hearing him cry got me worked up which meant I was also fully awake and really irritable. Preetam managed to put him back to sleep after a few minutes. After tossing and turning for what felt like ages, I also managed to fall back asleep.

4.30 am. Waah... Arjun was up again. I nudged Preetam who decided to go to the bathroom first (again) and Arjun woke up crying (again). I usually rushed to him the moment I heard him whine, maybe for selfish reasons, as maybe I didn't want to be fully awake. I felt frustrated.

Preetam ended up bringing Arjun into our bed. Again, frustrating, given how hard I had worked to break our co-sleeping habit (yes, I was THAT mum that vowed to never succumb to co-sleeping... ask me where he sleeps now 😊).

Maybe I was just using the above as an excuse to validate me feeling so crappy. Maybe it was actually *my* inability to deal with the unknown. My anxiety made me snappy. I felt sick when I thought about returning to work. "How long are they going to be patient with my baby brain? What if I cry in front of them? Would I remember how to do anything?" I hate change. I hate uncertainty and I hated the thought of being away from Arjun for about eight hours a day while at work. He'd be spending more time with nursery staff than with me.

My thoughts were interrupted by the sound of my alarm. And so, day one of my new reality began…

After getting ready and getting our "first day of nursery" snaps done, we set off. I got to nursery at 7.29 am bang on—I was gloating at my triumph of getting there a minute ahead of schedule.

I got out of the car and scooped him out of his car seat and hugged him tightly. My smile had been replaced with floods of tears. Arjun and I both cried inconsolably when I dropped him off. I sat in my car outside the nursery as I tried to calm myself down. I felt so empty and disconnected from who I was again. I wanted to be a mum, not an employee. Could I be both?

I arrived at work 25 minutes earlier than when I had planned on meeting my boss. It felt really strange pulling up into the work car park. It almost felt unfamiliar. I grabbed my pass and decided to get a coffee—it felt like a treat!

I placed my pass in the top-up machine to check how much credit I had—£2.10. That would be enough for a coffee but it wouldn't be enough for lunch. I reached into my handbag to grab some money. I couldn't feel it.

Panic.

"Where the heck is my purse? Crap, I must have left it on my dresser last night!!! What am I going to do?!" I texted Preetam in a panic. He reminded me there was a note I'd left in the car the other day. Phew!

I quickly rushed back to the car then topped up my card and grabbed a coffee.

I made a quick call to Arjun's nursery to see if he was okay and felt instant relief on hearing the friendly voice at the other end of the line. She said he was okay and had finished off his breakfast and was now playing outside. I felt calmer.

I reached into my bag to email my boss to let him know I was here. Where is my blackberry? Oh my goodness, what a terrible first impression I'm going to make! I'd left it on charge at home and had forgotten to pick it up on my way out!

At that same moment, the lady at reception asked, "Are you Harps?" Turns out my boss had asked her to look out for me. Phew.

And that was that; I re-entered the world of Finance. The morning in general wasn't too bad. I had three meetings and felt pretty positive about my role. My new team were all lovely and two of the others had also recently had babies. My boss had been great at making me feel comfortable and had walked me through things from a top-level overview.

By lunchtime, I felt exhausted. I called Arjun's nursery while grabbing a bite to eat. They said Preetam had also called. They said Arjun had been really good and he'd had two lots of lunches! That's my boy!

I had a few more meetings, managed to get my laptop sorted and cleared my inbox as well as doing a few admin bits.

I couldn't wait to collect Arjun but the drive there felt so long especially as I struggled to keep my eyes open!

As I pulled up outside the nursery, I felt a new lease of life. I jumped out of the car and literally ran down the corridor. As I entered his room, I could see he was nodding off. He was sitting with a member of staff who was patting him on his back to put him to sleep. I watched him for a few minutes as he lay there peacefully. I then crouched down next to him and as soon as he saw me, he shot up and came crawling over at full speed and cried and cried. He hugged me so tight. It felt so nice to have my baby in my arms again. I held him tight to reassure him that I wasn't going anywhere. I took as much comfort in him as he took in me. The staff said he'd had a really good first day and that he seemed to be settling in well and had formed a special bond with Becca (one of the nursery nurses)—he played with her and cried when she left the room but was comforted when she cuddled him on her return. I took relief in knowing that he felt comfortable with someone there when I was not around.

The staff were incredibly sweet—Becca had put together a collage of pictures from Arjun's first day with cute captions. A perfect little keepsake of Arjun's first day at nursery.

I tried to put Arjun into his car seat but he cried frantically. I patiently took him out and cuddled him a few times. I wanted him to feel reassured that I was there for him. I felt extra-sensitive to his feelings.

When we got home, Arjun and I played. I found the energy from somewhere. I wanted to make the most of every single minute I had with him.

Arjun & I enjoying a post work/nursery snack

When Arjun heard his daddy walk through the front door, he shot over to him and embraced his papa like I'd never seen. He kept cuddling him and burying his head in his neck and then lifting his head up to keep checking that it really was his daddy. It made me well up. I could see how emotional Preetam was too.

The two of them played with a football for a while before Arjun had his dinner, bath and milk. He fell asleep within a few minutes of us cuddling. It was the perfect end to my first day back to work.

As time went on, I settled into my role at work. Arjun still cried every morning and every evening on pick-up for his entire first year. It hurt but I knew he was okay during the day. We settled into our new routine and found our own way.

Between being a mummy, working, and enjoying life, I felt calmer and more content.

CHAPTER 11:

Baby Number 2

WE'D ALWAYS WANTED ANOTHER baby, God willing, more for Arjun than for ourselves. Both Preetam and I have two siblings and have grown up in busy homes. We wanted that same hustle and bustle in our own house— that same feeling of having your best friends at home. Arjun was just over one and it felt like the right time.

We had dreams.

We had hopes.

We fell pregnant instantly with Arjun and I guess we'd assumed the same would happen the second time round. Perhaps we took it for granted?

It didn't.

Each month, I'd go in filled with hope. I had my routine of taking a pregnancy test the day before my period was due—I'm sure some of you reading this can relate. Like me, I'm sure there are many women who have a drawer dedicated to ovulation kits and pregnancy tests while riding the journey of conception. I became so obsessed with the mechanics that I ended up spending a fortune on tests—so much so that I had to switch from the premium brands to the cheaper eBay ones as it was becoming an expensive habit! Each time, I'd pray for a positive test and each month, a single stripe would appear—sometimes I thought I was going crazy and wondered if I could very faintly see another. But of course, it was my mind playing tricks on me.

As each month brought with it fading hope and a negative pregnancy test, the desire to want another baby mounted and the frustration around not understanding why it wasn't happening grew. My judgement was clouded—I wasn't even sure anymore if it was because I wanted another baby or if it was because I felt like I was failing. I blamed my body for failing us in being able to conceive again. As I pondered over the reason, my attention was diverted from focusing on the baby that I did have. Arjun was at such a fun playful age but my mind was often preoccupied.

Every time I heard the news that someone was pregnant, my heart sank. It wasn't that I was unhappy for them, it was just that I so badly wanted it for us too. When would it happen for us? I had to catch myself and remind myself that what was written for us, would eventually find us. I felt selfish and ungrateful—we already had Arjun but I couldn't help but yearn to give him a sibling.

In April of 2016, I was pretty engrossed with Amrit's wedding. I was grateful to have a distraction, to not be so fixated on having a baby. I enjoyed dressing up and riding the emotions of this new journey alongside my best friend.

I wanted to absorb each and every emotion she was feeling along with her as I knew it all too well from my time. The day of her wedding was an emotional one; Indian weddings always are! I woke up the next morning and realised it was a day after my period was due. I'd taken a First Response test a few days earlier which promises to show a result up to five days before a missed period and it had come back negative. I was convinced that this month, I was definitely not pregnant as the odds weren't really in our favour.

Preetam was outside painting our fence, and Arjun and I were having morning snuggles when I decided to do a cheap test out of force of habit. It had become a ritual—something that I just did. I did my thing of peeing on a stick and then cracked on with putting away the outfits from the night before.

I wandered back into the bathroom prepared to throw away yet another pregnancy test—I had become conditioned to expect failure amidst the bouts of hope.

Two pink lines!

I was completely shocked when I saw a faint second pink line! Had I left the test out too long and therefore it was giving me a false positive? I decided to use the last Clearblue Test I had to double-check… I was so surprised to see a positive after seeing negatives a few days before! I embraced Arjun and cried. I handed him the stick (after wiping it with a Dettol wipe as you do!) and rushed down to show it to Preetam who was equally as surprised and thrilled! I felt relieved. It was the day of my best friend's wedding reception and it was the most perfect day for so many reasons!

Nine months—the time I thought I'd have a new baby in my arms is how long it took us to conceive. It was okay though; it had finally happened and I felt immensely grateful.

Those dreams and hopes Preetam and I had of growing our family began to become a reality. I could picture it—it was so real I could almost touch it. The thought of our family growing made my heart swell.

I'd done it all before with Arjun, but this time, having something go wrong with my child wasn't at the forefront of my mind in the same way it was with him. It was going to be perfect; we were going to be perfect. Everything was going to be great!

We shared the news with our families by putting Arjun in a "Baby Brother arriving December 2016" t-shirt and took him to both houses. They were really excited to be welcoming another addition. It was doubly exciting as Preetam's sister, Mané, was also pregnant, due just a few weeks before me! We enjoyed planning what life with the babies would be once they'd arrived, comparing cravings and aversions and just having each other.

With the amazing pregnancy news, I was also nominated for an award. Unbelievably, I won Best Preschool Blog 2016 in the Mum & Dad Awards (MAD Blog Awards). I was completely blown away! Following my win, Arjun and I were featured in our local newspaper and we were also invited to speak on the BBC Asian Network radio station. I felt so happy and that things were really going our way.

Arjun & I at the BBC Asian Network studios

My bubble soon popped.

I was six weeks pregnant and I woke up to the sight of blood in my pants. Not a lot, but still visible nonetheless. I reminded myself that I'd had a small bleed with Arjun too and that it turned out okay but I knew, truthfully, it wasn't a great sign. I felt sick with fear. We'd waited for what felt like ages and now that I'd had a taste of our future, I was terrified that we were going to be robbed of it.

We were told to visit the Early Pregnancy Unit. Here, we were ushered into a private room and we were told to prepare ourselves as I may have an ectopic pregnancy. We were asked to return in a week to see if the pregnancy was viable.

We left silently, without uttering a word to each other.

How had our lives gone from hopes and dreams to fear and dread in just a week?

That week was the longest of my life. It didn't help that Preetam and I have very different ways of dealing with stress. He switches off and internalises his worries and I'm a talker. The happy and beautiful start of this pregnancy that I'd hoped for was short lived.

That week was absolute torture and I felt so alone. I struggled to function, I had no energy and I shut off from the world. That one week of torture felt like a lifetime. I felt stressed by Arjun and his needs as I was consumed with dread that there would be no second baby.

We revisited a week later almost prepared for the worst. I had no glimmer of hope.

As the sonographer placed the probe on my belly, there was a tiny flicker!

"Congratulations", she said. My eyes filled up—our baby was safe and hope was reignited. Preetam let out a sigh of relief.

Despite the happy news, the week had felt so poignant. I couldn't seem to shake it off and that feeling spilled into the next nine months.

I found myself in a dark space quite quickly. It was something I almost resented myself for. I was so mindful and aware of how lucky I was to even be pregnant again and feeling melancholy made me frustrated and irritated with myself—it didn't help as it results in a vicious cycle. I had to constantly remind myself to not compare my situation to others and beat myself up for feeling rubbish some days as everyone's situation is very relevant and real to them.

I was going to reach the 12-week mark around the time of Arjun's second birthday, so we decided to get a private scan done at Harley Street to ensure all was "okay" before sharing the news with our wider family and friends, especially as I was showing a lot earlier. My NHS scan date was after the date of his birthday party. Looking back, I'm not sure what "okay" even meant. It was kind of a tick box exercise, a safety check almost. We had a one in 100,000 *"risk"* of having a child with any genetic abnormality. All was fine and I was okay to share the news wider.

Despite all being "okay", I still struggled to shake off the sadness I was feeling.

Some days I didn't even have the energy to speak.
Some days I'd wake up feeling fine.
Some days all I needed was to be left alone.
Some days I'd wake up forgetting I was even pregnant.
Some days I'd wake up feeling excited at the prospect.
Some days I'd spend the day dwelling on things so

much so that I'd get confused between reality and those things that were a figment of my imagination.

Some days I couldn't get out of bed.

Somme days all I needed was a hug.

Some days I'd work myself up so much that I'd end up having a panic attack—something that was new to me.

Some days Paw Patrol was on for a lot longer than it should have been.

Some days I felt so anxious but nothing and no one could help.

Some days I could sleep the whole day; other days I struggled to even fall asleep.

None of my feelings were directly related to my unborn baby. "How can I feel so sad at one of the happiest times of our lives?" I'd wonder. I felt ungrateful and so resentful towards myself. But I also felt a little sorry for myself; I felt stuck. Every so often, the devil on my shoulder would show up rearing its ugly head.

I'd often be consumed by a cloud of sadness and I'd have no real understanding of why. This isn't how I imagined my second pregnancy to be. I was so excited at the prospect of being pregnant and don't get me wrong, I couldn't wait to grow our family and for Arjun to be a big brother, I just didn't feel how I expected to feel. I wanted to be bouncy and happy, I wanted to be busy coming up with a plan of baby groups I was keen on attending, I wanted to be eagerly shopping, writing to my baby—all the things I did with my first pregnancy, but I didn't.

Admittedly, we had had a hell of a lot of change happening in our lives at the time; a new baby on the way and an extension to our house that was in full swing. Preetam and I decided it would be best for Arjun and I to move to my parents once I'd hit the 12-week mark while the building work was carried out. I was unable to prepare the baby's clothes as our house was full of dust and wasn't anywhere near being in order yet. I had no idea if all the changes happening were causing so much disruption for me mentally or if this was always going to be the case.

I was more realistic with this pregnancy and wasn't walking on air as I was when pregnant with Arjun; I was very aware of PND and what could happen, but this time, I was equipped. As I was diagnosed with PND early on post-birth with Arjun, this time around it was picked up on my first midwife appointment. If you've had it before, you're at a higher risk of having it again. I had a mental health midwife support me through my pregnancy. Over 27,000 people subscribe to the Pandas Foundation (Pre and Post-Natal Depression Advice & Support) on Facebook which shows just how many others are in a similar position to what I was.

After my initial midwife appointment, I was referred to the antenatal psychiatrist to be assessed. Where before the word "psychiatrist" would have freaked me out, I knew it didn't have the stigma attached to it that some people may associate with it, especially in my culture— it just meant I needed a little bit of help and support and she'd be the best-placed person to decide what that support should be.

I met her and we had a chat. I cried, I laughed, she rode my emotions with me and then we agreed on a plan of action going forward. I'd had counselling previously, both after my car accident and when I had Arjun, and I knew that rather than cognitive behaviour therapy (CBT), talking therapy works best for me. Sometimes, I just need to air out my emotions and feelings to an independent impartial party to rationalise my thoughts. I was referred to a company called "Talking Therapies" which works for the NHS with those who may be in a similar situation to me. I was contacted very quickly by them and began weekly counselling sessions over the phone; something I was so grateful they offered. The thought of having to drive anywhere or arrange childcare for Arjun would have put me off. I found the sessions so therapeutic and relieving. I was able to cry and talk about my weekly worries and stresses, and simply speaking about them helped. My counsellor was lovely and so supportive. I also continued to be supported by the mental health midwife appointments.

After a few sessions, I was invited to a well-being group at the hospital. I was really apprehensive about going. I didn't feel like facing anyone but I managed to force myself to go. The class consisted of about eight other people; many women had bought their partners along—something I wish I'd done with Preetam for him to understand my psyche a little more. We went through the different types of stress and worry, the reaction to stress and anxiety and relaxation techniques such as breathing exercises, mindfulness and imagery therapy.

After the well-being class, I was contacted by Talking Therapies again who recommended face-to-face counselling. Fortunately, my GP surgery is on the same street as my house so it didn't mean I had to go far.

My last pregnancy was so different. I felt happy, excited and elated. I'm not sure if knowing how I felt post-birth last time had scarred me and tainted my view somewhat and was what was making this pregnancy much harder, or perhaps I was just not giving myself enough credit for all the change I was also experiencing, the guilt surrounding Arjun, and the lack of stability.

Coming to stay at my parents' house definitely made a difference. Perhaps I needed a change of scenery and to focus on myself for a little while, almost to recharge my batteries, clear my mind and be fed my favourite foods! I made time to connect with the baby blossoming inside of me—I was more mindful than the first time and was also fearful of not having a connection with this one when he or she was born.

It was also great for Arjun to spend quality time with his Nana Ji, Nani Ji and masis. My dad was determined to get Arjun potty trained before the baby arrived and with his perseverance (and an army to make it happen), we managed to do it! Arjun loved spending time with his Nana Ji in the garden. He also looked forward to walking Chico with my dad each morning. He had ample opportunity to do painting and crafts with his masis and got fed his favourite foods made by Nani.

Deep in conversation with Nana Ji

One afternoon, my Suzi Thai Ji (my dad's brother's wife) came over to spend some time with me and to show us her new car. I was really close to her. I found her non-Asian mentality refreshing. I would often stay the night at their house when I was little. She'd lovingly coined me her "kadhu"; Punjabi for "pumpkin". Though she was English, I admired how much effort she'd poured into learning about our culture. Her love story to my Thaia Ji (uncle) was epic and despite their hurdles, they tackled the world. They married in the 1960s when it was quite unthinkable for an Asian man to marry an English woman and when overt racism was at its peak.

I'd often share things with her, and, despite the age difference of almost 50 years, she felt like a friend. She was someone that I laughed with, cried with, took comfort in, and someone who gave me so much strength. Throughout most of her life, she suffered with ill health, yet, she continued to have a bright smile on her pretty face. She was someone who lived life like there was no tomorrow but dreamt like she had forever.

She always had her hair and nails done and was always donning some form of leopard print! She'd wear her Indian gold earrings and a spectacular choice of one of her 500 pairs of shoes on! She always dressed well and embraced the Indian culture too; "I'm not gori (English), I'm Indian." she'd say.

Given I'd spent so much time with them growing up, she'd share so many childhood memories with me. She'd laugh just as hard every time she told them. Her favourite was the one about me shouting "Donald's" every time we drove past McDonald's and how I would give all the shorter chips to them but keep the longer ones for myself (some things never change!). She was always so proud of me and referred to me as a daughter.

I loved receiving her text messages; they were always filled with grand news or something super exciting. The most recent was her excitement at buying a new car, an old school Rolls Royce, and that's what she'd come over to show us.

I enjoyed spending the afternoon with her, laughing and joking. She told me to plan a date night with Heera (she always referred to him by his nickname) and to make the most of our time. I obliged. Preetam and I went to the cinema the next evening while my parents and sisters took care of Arjun; a rare break for us from the pressure of work and the extension. Preetam was also really fond of my Thai Ji and her playful nature. We spoke about her a lot while enjoying dinner at a Greek restaurant.

That night, we got back to my parents and were still laughing, joking and enjoying each other's company downstairs when my sisters and parents came down. It was 11 pm. They'd usually be fast asleep. Why were they awake?

"We have something to tell you", they said.

"What?" we said.

"Suzi's gone", they said.

"Suzi's gone where?!" I asked confused.

"She's gone Harps."

WHAT?

How could this have happened? I was with her just the day before! How could she be gone? I never thought that would be the last time we'd meet.

Preetam and I had been speaking about her so much that night, but what we didn't realise was that at that same moment, she was slipping away and leaving us. The night was a blur but what I felt is still so vivid. Arjun had come down by this time to the sound of me hysterically sobbing, buried in Preetam's chest. He didn't know what to do; I couldn't even take any comfort in my son.

Why is the one thing that's guaranteed in life, death, so hard to accept?

I was so grateful to have Arjun by my side holding my hand through a rocky journey. I felt guilty whenever he witnessed me crying, that he had to carry the burden of that, but his sweet words of "mummy, no crying, cuddles", and the warmth of his embrace was and still is enough to restore in me the faith and belief that I *will* be okay.

I tried to focus on the beautiful picture that lay ahead (God willing):

A new baby
Our new humble castle
My family reunited
… a bright future.

I was thankful to Preetam for his patience as I rode rough emotions even when he found it difficult to understand. I felt grateful to my dearest friends Amrit and Sav for being my safe outlet and, of course, my family for always being there

Though I was under consultant-led care again this time, I wasn't as anxious about something going wrong. I had done it all before; it would be okay. Having a child already meant I didn't have much time to worry. Between running around after a toddler and managing my growing belly, as well as managing my day-to-day emotions, I was tired most of the time.

Not only did Arjun have to deal with the idea of a sibling, but we were also dealing with living apart from

Preetam, the impact of which I really underestimated. Though Preetam came to see us at least every other day, he didn't have as much time to spend with Arjun as he did before as we were frantically trying to get things done in time for the baby's arrival. Preetam was often working till past midnight straight after work before rising the next morning at 6 am to go to work before repeating the same day again. It was tough on all of us. We did schedule in family days in where possible but not being together everyday was tough on all of us.

Preetam, Arjun & I visiting Santa's grotto for Christmas

As well as the building work, Arjun also changed rooms at nursery, something that had taken him a long while to adapt to. The staff in his new room seemed a lot less invested which concerned me as I needed him to have a solid support system through all these changes. It was so upsetting to see him hysterical in the mornings, physically fighting to come back to me as I left him to go to work, and it just added to the guilt. I'd worry that he was unable to express what he was feeling and that he may have been carrying a heavy weight around.

His behaviour had definitely changed since we shared the news. He became a lot clingier, especially to me. Where he'd happily walk around before, most of the time now when we were out, he wanted me to pick him up. But I knew it was just a phase and his way of seeking reassurance. I wanted to be able to give him that as his mother. He became more affectionate and sometimes it felt as though he was scared of someone else taking me away from him. He was still so little himself.

I became so hyperaware that things were changing as our family was growing and that I wanted to implement the change in small stages if possible so Arjun didn't have to deal with too many things at once. I struggled with the change myself; I've always struggled with surrendering to change and embracing it.

I prayed that he didn't have to grow up too quickly. To me, he was still a baby; a tiny person with lots of emotions navigating his way through life. He'd be feeling emotions that he'd never felt before and that were alien to him, both positive and negative. I wanted to make sure I was giving him as much support to process those feelings and emotions as possible through Preetam and I holding his hand through this journey.

We asked the nursery to read lots of books to him about becoming a new brother. We also bought him a baby doll; sometimes he'd lovingly lull his baby doll to sleep and other times he'd go missing to find his screwdriver to screw the baby's eyes out! We also encouraged him to watch episodes of his favourite cartoons involving babies. One of Arjun's favourite episodes of *Mickey Mouse* was "Goofy Baby" where Goofy morphs into a baby and the rest of the crew have to babysit him. In that episode, they put Goofy to sleep, change his nappy, feed him and burp him and also try and settle him when he is crying. Arjun would then mimic with the baby doll what they did on the programmes.

I'd encourage Arjun to talk to the baby when he felt comfortable doing so but I never pushed him. He'd often say, "Wakey, wakey, baby!" while stroking my belly. I'd talk to him as much as possible about the baby without it being overwhelming and without every conversation being dominated by it. At the same time, I wanted to make the most of my time with him as a single child. We took Arjun shopping to pick out clothes for the baby; he was more interested in the escalator! For the birth of the baby, I let Arjun pick which matching leggings fabric he liked and made us all matching pairs as the baby's coming home outfit so Arjun felt very much included. I also got Arjun a gift from the baby for the first time he'd come to meet him or her.

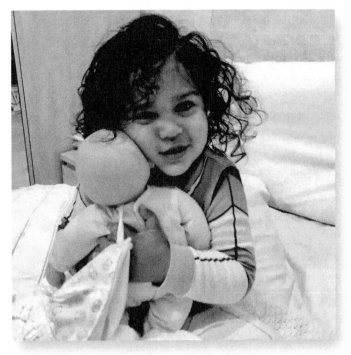

Arjun practising playing big brother with his own baby

Sometimes he'd stroke my belly, give it gentle kisses and rest his head on it while watching TV. He'd use my belly button as a peephole to see the baby and tell them he loved them so much which always melted me. Sometimes he'd acknowledge that there was a baby in mummy's tummy and boastfully tell other pregnant ladies with similar bellies that the baby was in his mummy's tummy. Other times he'd say there was no baby.

Sometimes he'd excitedly talk about the baby himself, and other times he'd have selective hearing and completely ignore you if you mentioned it.

Arjun's behaviour towards babies slowly started to change on the news of his baby brother or sister. He became sensitive to other babies and it felt like he'd developed a new sense of understanding and responsibility towards them. My cousin had recently had a baby and when baby Jaylen cried, Arjun would try and comfort him by telling him, "Mummy's coming". He also played very differently with babies, almost in an adult-like manner, where he'd try and explain to Jaylen what the toy was, how it worked and the sounds it made.

The more I watched him and heard his excitement, the more I became excited. He was at such a precious age—our favourite stage of his development where his vocabulary was rapidly increasing but it was still so cute and baby-like.

I tried my best to support him during lots of change and to help him be as confident as possible. I had no doubt that he'd be a loving, protective and affectionate big brother once the baby arrived.

I remember one evening, Arjun summoned Preetam and I to his bed. He was in a very sleepy state but babbling nevertheless (definitely my boy!). He started talking about "Arjy's baby"—I watched him as he lay there with a beaming smile on his face with his eyes shut talking about his baby brother or sister. I'd never seen him looking so content and fulfilled—I welled up. I didn't really think he thought much about the baby outside of when we brought the subject up. To hear him speak about "his" baby with such happiness melted my heart.

As he spoke about the baby, he mentioned random words like parks and aeroplanes. It felt like he was contemplating his future with a sibling. How beautiful.

Though we were eager to fall pregnant and mentally, I'd only geared myself up for all the positive feelings I thought I'd endure when we finally saw a big fat smiley on our pregnancy test. What I didn't realise was how consumed with guilt I would eventually be; the guilt of having another.

Arjun was at the most beautiful and captivating age at just over two years old. His innocence was still present, but his curiosity meant that he'd become a proper little person. He was a person who could voice his likes and dislikes, a person who could tell you how he was feeling most of the time, a person who oozed love and affection but also had the ability to turn into a little gizmo in a split second. This phase was undoubtedly my favourite. I cried on so many occasions at the thought of it disappearing as quickly as the last 27 months had. Is it bad that a part of me wished I could save my whole self to just observe and enjoy him growing up? I'd spend each and every day with him; but I still found everything he did so fascinating—I never ever got bored.

In that moment, he was the very centre of our world; at the heart of every single thing that we did. He got to have mummy and daddy's undivided attention. He was happiest when he had both of us around him; the smile on his face and the glimmer in his eye showed us how full and content he felt when we were both with him. Those few months that we lived apart from Preetam were tough.

He'd cry at night for his daddy and sometimes Preetam would drive from home to Southall just to put him to sleep.

With the baby due in a month and us potentially moving back by Christmas, I felt like he wasn't going to have any quality time with the two of us before the new arrival. "How will such a small human cope with the emotions he'll have to ride when it comes to sharing us with another tiny person? How is he going to process foreign feelings? What if he feels rejected? What if he feels like he wasn't enough for us and that is why we had to get another baby? What if he isn't able to express his emotions? What if he hates us? What if he becomes distant? I'm not sure I'll be able to cope with that." My heart felt so heavy.

At that moment, he was also the only grandchild on both sides and was showered with so much love and affection. As soon as he walked into his Dada Ji's (paternal grandparents) or Nana Ji's (maternal grandparents) house, all eyes were on him. Soon, on Preetam's side, there'd be three babies, and, on my side, there'd be two. Again, more change. Would he feel like he wasn't enough for everyone?

I knew it was a part of life and that he'd have a friend forever. I knew, eventually, he'd learn to love his sibling but what I felt so horribly guilty about was all the emotions and feelings this little person was going to have to ride through to get to that stage. I felt awful that he'd have to share us. We wouldn't always be able to drop everything for him.

My fear wasn't the tantrums and attention-seeking that may come my way, as I was half expecting that; I was more worried about his feelings and emotions. "Will he lose his happy spirit? Will his personality change? Will he have to grow up too quick? What if he wants a morning cuddle and I'm unable to because I'm too tired? Or because I'm feeding the baby? What if I'm unable to love two people as much as I love Arjun?"

I tried my best to get him used to the idea of a sibling, but if I couldn't fully comprehend it, how could I expect him to?

I tried harder to bond with this baby as I was worried the same thing would happen the second time around. I felt more maternal than I had with Arjun but it still felt strange. On the rare occasions when I'd have a moment of peace, I'd allow myself to get lost in dreaming about my two little humans running around in our dream home.

The pregnancy was quite different from my first but I've always heard that no two pregnancies are ever the same. I didn't gain as much weight; I had fewer cravings and more aversions with this pregnancy. I couldn't stand the smell of macaroni cheese or garlic bread (which was my favourite before falling pregnant!). I remember visiting my in-laws and my mother-in-law had made her signature macaroni cheese (she makes the best cheese sauce I've ever tasted!) and the smell alone made me vomit into my hands; classy!

I was really grateful to Mrs G, who continued to support me through my second pregnancy too. She was delighted when I requested her—she knew me and my irrationality all too well! I was given the option to come to day care, as I had done with my first pregnancy, more for reassurance, however, I opted out. I did end up visiting the hospital on numerous occasions as I hadn't felt much movement but was reassured by hearing my baby's heartbeat and the midwives' satisfaction with the cardiotocography (CTG) monitor which showed a steady heartbeat.

We discussed my labour options and I decided I'd like to try for a vaginal birth after C-section (VBAC). However, we scheduled a planned C-section for 39 weeks in case I didn't go into labour. It was booked in for 30th December.

By my third trimester, Arjun and I had been living at my parents' house for three months. It was a tough time. Being apart took its toll on us and it felt like we'd have to start as a family from scratch. But it was going to be perfect once we got back home.

CHAPTER 12:

A Guilty Heart

IT WAS JUST AFTER CHRISTMAS and our 2017 was about to start in the best way possible. We moved back home the day before I had my planned C-section. It felt strange coming back home especially as it looked so different; so much more open. I felt immensely grateful for the home we are blessed with but also for Preetam and how hard he worked on the renovations.

Everything felt so new and although it was newly furnished, it felt quite empty. Preetam has often said to me, "Harps, *you* make a house a home." and I couldn't wait to work my magic once I had the time, but for now, I had the urge to clean so that it was safe to welcome a newborn into. As Arjun ran around his new open-plan lounge, I rolled my sleeves up, got on my knees and began shining the glass on our lounge doors using good old Mr Muscle. I scanned the big clear space and the cream fluffy carpet that looked like a sea of calm and reminded me so much of my parents' home. The huge bifold doors that boasted a beautiful view of our garden felt inviting and I couldn't wait for the summer! I felt excited but overwhelmed. I wanted everything to be perfect for our new addition but time felt scarce. They'd be here within 24 hours!

As I was due a planned C-section, I was asked to carb-load the night before to ensure my energy reserves were up as I would be nil by mouth from midnight. I wasn't going to argue with that request especially given my first birth experience! We had a feast of pizza and chips from my favourite local takeaway. Indy also joined us as we laughed and joked. I felt grateful to be surrounded by family.

Knowing we'd be saying goodbye to Arjun that evening made me feel nervous. He had been my comfort and my guide—I didn't want to be away from him. I wrote a blog post that day to capture how I was feeling:

"I know I should be thinking about the bubbly and exciting times ahead, but before that, I know I have to do one of the hardest things I'll have to do… give my first-born the "last hug" before coming home with his sibling.

It isn't actually the last hug; there'll be so many more.

But it's the last one before he is no longer the only child.

The last one before our attention becomes divided. I don't want to say our love becomes divided; I want to believe that our love will simply grow to accommodate two little humans.

The last one before we become a family of four.

The last one before he is no longer the smallest person in our life.

Why do I feel so guilty? I feel guilty because I don't feel like he understands despite the countless number of times we've read "There's A House Inside My Mummy", despite the number of babies he's cooed over, despite the number of conversations we've had about it. I feel like it's some sort of betrayal; that we've made such a huge decision without his consent, without his knowledge, that he may feel like he's not enough.

I feel guilty because he won't be a part of those initial moments when the baby is born and that he'll be oblivious to the chaos that will no doubt be unfolding at the labour ward as he is left with his masis to be entertained (or to entertain!) and will go about his day laughing and playing like it's just any other without realising how much his life is about to change.

How will I face giving him that last hug? How will I stop my tears from flowing? As challenging as it has been, I have loved being a mummy to only him. I have loved the uninterrupted cuddles, the long random conversations and enjoying as many precious moments as I possibly could. You'd think living with him, I'd get bored of his antics—never. I laugh just as hard each time he does something funny; I find him fascinating. He has helped me overcome so much in the last few years and has been my biggest source of comfort and my strongest pillar of support—I hope I'm not hurting him. I hope he embraces me as tightly as he always has even when there's another.

I feel like that "last hug" will signify so much— the biggest thing it'll signify is "change"; a word that always sends me into a panic. I don't want anything to change with Arjun.

I know I'll embrace him as tightly as possible with tears streaming at the feel of his tiny little heartbeat against mine; one that he still takes comfort in… I know I'll be breaking inside and I won't want to let go and I won't want that little moment to end as it signifies so much. I write this behind misty eyes as I struggle to catch my breath; a moment that signifies the end of one chapter; a chapter that has filled my life and heart with so much joy.

I won't get to enjoy every single moment of either child as I know, at times, things will be crazy with a newborn crying and a toddler having a tantrum. But I also know there'll be many joyful moments."

Beep, beep.

Harv and Goov pulled up on our driveway a little after 9 pm to collect Arjun. He was staying there for the night while I gave birth to his sibling—my sisters are the closest thing to me that he has. I reluctantly gathered his overnight bag, placed him in his car seat and kissed him goodbye. As I looked into his innocent little eyes with tears flowing and my heart feeling torn, I felt guilt.

"The last hug"

The next time I'd see him next to a baby, he'd feel so grown up. I wanted to keep him as my precious little boy forever. I wasn't sure I wanted to share my love between two children. My heart was so full of love for him, how on earth could I ever love like this again? I didn't have the capacity.

"Bye, mummy and daddy!" He waved excitedly. I closed the door and the tears came harder and faster as I waved my little boy goodbye when they reversed out of our drive. I felt consumed by sadness at the thought of the change that was coming our way. As much as I wanted this, I felt comfortable in the familiarity of Arjun.

I didn't feel like cleaning anymore; I felt emotionally drained. As Preetam and I sat on the floor in our brand-new decorated lounge, we looked at each other with a little heartache in our eyes. "Something's going to go wrong." he said. He spoke the words I was feeling—"I think something's going to happen to me." I said.

Chapter 13:

Bliss… Finally!

That night, we put our heads down at about midnight. My bags were packed—they were considerably lighter than the first time around when I'd packed like I was off for a week in the Bahamas!

1 am. OUCH! Holy smokes, what on earth is that intense pain?!! I was woken by a contracting pain in my abdomen.

"Are these contractions or Braxton Hicks?" I asked myself. I didn't want to disturb Preetam if it was a false alarm knowing how tired he was. I hadn't gone into labour naturally the first time so was inexperienced in knowing what "real" labour felt like. The contractions became more frequent and more intense. I rang the maternity Triage, the hospital maternity helpline for pregnant ladies, who advised me to come in straight away due to being high risk.

I had a quick shower and woke Preetam. He was exhausted. We were knackered before our ordeal had even begun. He loaded the car with my bags and we made our way to the hospital. As I looked out of the car window at the world asleep, so still and clear, I felt a sense of calm.

I felt somewhat delirious from the tiredness. It felt almost like a dream; I couldn't believe this was actually happening! From nine months earlier, our happy ending was finally on its way.

On arriving at Triage, I was so pleased to see Danielle and Manjit—two lovely midwives that I had got to know well during my day care visits while I was pregnant with Arjun. I silently thanked God for the two familiar and warm faces that greeted me and that it wasn't busy.

It felt nice to have a brief distraction from the pain as we had a little catch-up and a few laughs. Seeing them, I felt comfort.

After a few minutes, Danielle connected me to the CTG monitor and confirmed that I was indeed in labour. Three contractions within 10 minutes. "What do you want to do, Harps?" she asked. I wondered if this was God's way of giving me the opportunity to experience a natural labour—something that I had longed to do.

"If I'm dilating, I'd love to try for natural labour." I replied. I prayed that I was and that it wasn't round two of what happened with Arjun where I was contracting but not dilating.

Danielle took me to an examination room; I performed the familiar task of popping my shoes off and climbing up onto the hospital bed as I stretched my legs apart for Danielle to examine. No shyness, no shame, it had become second nature while pregnant!

Danielle performed an internal examination, the discomfort drowned out by the contractions. "You're about half a centimetre", she said with a slight look of dismay.

I knew there and then, based on my previous experience, that I couldn't put myself through trying for a natural labour again if my body wasn't responding. I knew the exhaustion from the labour had contributed to my PND and I wanted to limit myself from that trauma as much as I was able to.

"Let's go for the C-section." I replied.

"This time, I'm coming with you! I'll get my scrubs ready!" Danielle replied excitedly. I felt instant comfort at the thought of her being by my side. I didn't feel guilty at the thought of a C-section like I had the last time.

The contractions were coming more intensely and more frequently. I sat waiting to go in for our C-section and had begun writing my birth story and how perfectly it was all going. I felt so happy, so content. Life felt so good. The chaos of the last few months and living apart was all coming together; it suddenly all felt worth it. Things were falling into place. This was how I'd imagined it. It was the first time in what felt like ages that Preetam and I had been alone—the last time being our cinema date the night Suzi Thai Ji had passed away. I felt safe with him by my side.

It was now 4 am and Preetam had fallen asleep on the hospital seat. I wondered if he'd be as great a father to his second-born as he had been to Arjun. How would it change me? How would I feel?

*Preetam & I eagerly awaiting
the arrival of our second baby*

6 am. Danielle entered and told us that an emergency case had taken priority and that there'd be a further wait. Her son had a dental appointment that she had to take him to so she had to leave at 7.30 am. I was gutted. We hadn't anticipated that we'd be waiting so long but still, I trusted that all was working out just the way it was meant to!

8.20 am. The midwives arrived—it was my turn! I was so excited!

As I was taken into theatre, I was suddenly stricken with panic at the thought of the epidural; the nightmare of my first labour came flooding back. I cried before they'd even inserted the needle as I allowed the past to enter my present and paralyse me with fear. My head sank into Preetam's chest and he embraced me tightly. The empathetic consultant took extra care and I held my breath and clenched my fists as he began to administer. Thankfully, this time it worked the first time.

I lay down to get myself comfortable. A planned C-section is considerably different to an emergency C-section. I remember the chaos, the number of people in theatre and the fast pace of Arjun's delivery. This felt calm. Everything was explained to me.

They began poking and prodding and I could feel every single sensation—"STOP!" I screamed. I didn't recall being able to feel anything the last time. They administered more anaesthetic. I could still feel everything. "Harps, we've got one more dose left before we're left with no choice but to put you under general anaesthetic."

"No", I thought, "I can't miss those initial moments of my baby being born again."

Thankfully, the third shot numbed the sensation enough to a bearable state though still not as much as my first pregnancy. Perhaps I was more aware? Had I known what to expect?

As I settled down for my C-section, the gentle soothing sound of Simran played in the background; a sound my baby was so familiar with that I began to feel calmer.

9.32 am on 30th December 2016: I was made whole.

Saajan Singh was born and he came out screaming.

"I miss Arjun" were the first words that Preetam uttered. I didn't understand why at the time. I almost bit his head off and said, "What are you talking about?! We'll see Arjun soon! Focus on your new son."

Immediately after he was born, he was taken by the midwife who checked him over. To be honest, I was oblivious to what the normal protocol was after having a baby as I passed out right after delivering Arjun.

What felt like a few minutes later, Saajan was placed in my arms. I didn't notice anything different about him other than his fingernails being longer than Arjun's had been when he was born.

He was just a baby. My baby. He was just Saajan.

Bliss; this is what I'd imagined.

It was perfect.

I sat with Preetam in the recovery room with Saajan lying on my chest; I felt the most comforting sound of our heartbeats syncing and he took to my breast like a duck to water. A midwife commented to another midwife about how good that was; little did I know why. Of course, I felt like a super-proud mama and was pretty chuffed with myself for nailing it with Saajan right away, oblivious to why they were saying it.

I looked at Preetam and said, "I've never felt this happy and complete before", as I breastfed Saajan in my euphoric state.

He responded with silence.

I remember Preetam pointing out that Saajan's profile was different to his own and Arjun's as he faffed about with picture angles whilst taking a photo of Saajan to send to our family. I became quite defensive. I felt as though he was trying to say something negative... It was his way of gently trying to prepare me for what he already knew.

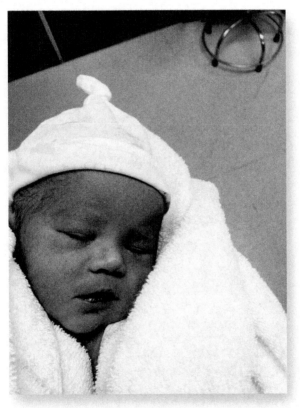

Saajan Singh—the picture that was sent to our loved ones to share the news of our new baby

Other than that, I remember very little detail about what happened in the initial few hours after Saajan was born. I don't remember how I was taken from the recovery room to the labour ward. I don't remember what my first meal after delivery was. I don't remember what Saajan's first outfit was. The only thing I remember is how I *felt*. Whole.

As the day passed, I was excited for Arjun to meet his brother and for our families to meet our new little guy. Preetam had already sent the family a picture of him.

Arjun meeting his new baby brother

My sisters arrived armed with balloons and with my precious first-born who was armed with a gift for his baby brother—a cute baby blue giraffe plush.

"Mummy, he's so cute." he said as he gently stroked his little face. It was beautiful and my heart was absolutely bursting with joy. My beautiful perfect family. I cried happy tears as I scanned Arjun's beautiful face cooing over his brother; he didn't look small anymore compared

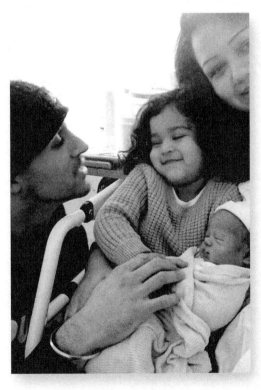

Our first picture as a family of four

to a newborn; he looked so grown up. We had waited for this day and now it was finally here.

It was about 7 pm and Preetam and Harv went to get us some food. Our families had started arriving but they were waiting outside as we were only allowed two visitors at a time. Goov was with me. There was a knock at our door. It was the Paediatrician. She examined Saajan while I gloated to Goov about how happy I was. Dr C asked, "Is your husband here?" I was in such a happy bubble that I thought nothing of it as I embraced the euphoria.

"He's gone to get food", I replied. She asked me to call him so I did…

CHAPTER 14:

What?

PREETAM RAN BACK. I GUESS he had been anticipating this moment from the time Saajan was born but he was probably hoping that it was just an intrusive odd thought as opposed to a potential reality. The doctor asked the others to leave the room.

"Do you notice anything different about your son? Does he look different to your other son?" she asked.

"He has Down's syndrome." replied Preetam abruptly.

The room froze.

Silence.

My head started spinning. I sank down into the bed as the dizziness distorted my balance and the blood rushed to my head.

The conversation from the night before flashed before my eyes. Intuition.

My mind went blank.

What on earth was Preetam talking about?! Has he gone crazy?

"I'm so sorry", she said as she looked down, unsure how else to respond to the sheer shock and devastation on our faces. The trail of her sentence was cut off by the sound of Preetam bursting into uncontrollable sobs. I'd never seen him like this.

I scanned my hands confused by what was going on around me. I was surprisingly calm, numb, in shock.

Was this a horrible nightmare?

Everything started happening fast—my brain wasn't able to process it as quickly as it was unfolding. My heart was racing at the same pace.

I wanted to scream but no sound came out. I wanted to cry but no tears flowed. Preetam let out a loud cry from the pit of his stomach—his distress at the news being expressed in full force. My adrenaline kicked in and I embraced him in my arms as I lay in my bed still recovering from the C-section. I was shell-shocked. What the hell was going on?

"It's okay. It's okay. It's okay." I repeated as I rocked back and forth with my arms around him. "It's okay. It's okay." I tried to convince myself as the rational part of my brain tried to take control. I felt like a robot programmed to say the right thing.

For Preetam, it was confirmation of what he had thought. It was reality staring him in the face. For me, it was the shock. Of his reaction. Of the diagnosis. Of my new reality. I had no idea. I felt like an outsider looking in. Looking back now at the pictures, you can see as clear as day that Saajan had Down's syndrome by his physical characteristics—I can see what Preetam saw. I was just so overwhelmed with my bursting love that I didn't notice at the time.

A wave of fear washed over me as my mind was clouded with judgement and prejudice; my misconception led to me having a prominent image of a "forever baby", being dependent on us for the rest of his life.

My thoughts were interrupted by Preetam's loud sobs as Dr C stood there speechless. "I'm so sorry", she uttered again. I wished she'd just go away.

The world seemed to be whizzing by me. Conversations sounded like buzzing bees in the background as I zoned out the noise and got lost in a fuzzy bubble—was this really happening?

I felt faint and confused.

I suddenly felt very tired.

How could I have been feeling like I was walking on air just moments before?

The room felt like it was zoning out. What was happening? This must be some kind of mistake!? All my scans had come back low risk; I'd had over twelve scans by six different sonographers. I'd paid for my nuchal test and anomaly at Harley Street. Both the NHS and Harley Street confirmed I had a one in 100,000 *risk* of having a baby with any condition. She was WRONG.

One in every 1,000 babies is born with Down's syndrome—that's 750 born in the UK each year. Was I really the mother of one of them?

She told us they'd carry out blood tests to confirm Trisomy 21. Maybe the results would reveal that he didn't have Down's syndrome? The doctor told us he definitely did and that there was only a five percent chance that he didn't; she told us the bloods were just a mere formality. She said we could share the news with our loved ones. I hated the doctor. I hated her for ruining my life. It was her who had torn our "perfect" family apart.

The baby, who had brought me so much joy just a minute ago, felt like a complete stranger. They'd described it as a risk factor when I was pregnant. Would he be a danger to me?! Did he pose a threat to the family? Why was it described as a risk?! I needed to know *what* this meant for us. Why was Dr C "sorry"? What did that mean?

Our parents hadn't even met Saajan yet. They were eagerly waiting outside to come in. How were we going to break the news to our families? My Arjun! How would my Arjun feel? How would he cope?! What was our future going to be? What had we done?! My perfect family had slipped through my fingers.

We were handed a heartless leaflet that told us our son had a 15 percent increased chance of leukaemia—it felt like the aim of all of this was to torture us. As I scanned the face of the little boy on the leaflet, my heart sank. As beautiful as he was, at that time, I didn't want a child "like that".

Our parents and siblings entered the room.

Before anyone was even to see Saajan, between sobs, Preetam blurted out, "He has Down's syndrome."

The room fell silent as our parents took a moment to process if they had definitely heard what they thought they'd heard.

Suddenly, the room felt chaotic as the delay in reaction passed. My mother-in-law almost fainted at the sight of her son in such a vulnerable state; the son who didn't often show emotion. My father-in-law left stunned. My mum had silent tears rolling down her cheeks as she looked at me, helpless and shocked. I clearly remember my dad holding Saajan and the colour from his face washing away as he absorbed what he was being told; shock. And in the middle of it stood Arjun, probably trying to make sense and understand what was going on and why everyone was crying when he was feeling so happy that he had a little baby brother. This was the happiest day of his life, so why was everyone so sad?

"Mummy, I love him." he whispered as he held his baby brother and gazed into his eyes, pride bursting from him. I felt devastated looking at him; we were meant to give him a best friend but instead, at that time, I felt like I had birthed a burden. I remembered the blog post I had written just the night before—*"That he'll be oblivious to the chaos that will no doubt be unfolding in the labour ward as he is left with his masis to be entertained (or to entertain!) and will go about his day laughing and playing…"*—I had no idea just what that chaos was going to be.

Would I be blamed for this? I carried him. Maybe I hadn't taken care of myself properly. Maybe it was karma. What would my in-laws think? Would this pan out like a *Star Plus* drama where I'd be ridiculed for life for birthing such a child? Would he ever be loved? How would my parents deal with people's perceptions? I wondered if our parents would rather I had birthed a fit and healthy girl over a disabled son. Or was it still preferred to have a boy despite what complications came with it? I didn't blame them though; it's all part of the social conditioning that they've endured.

It's crazy to think my biggest worry just 24 hours earlier was the method of delivery.

And just like that, what was meant to be the start of a beautiful 2017 was the start of a horrific year as we began to grieve for the child that we thought we were going to have. With that comes its own guilt.

I clutched on so tightly to that five percent; that the doctors would be proved wrong through his bloods, praying and hoping that it wouldn't be true.

CHAPTER 15:

The Greatest Storm

PREETAM STAYED WITH ME AT the hospital for the first night while my sisters took care of Arjun at home and protected him from the chaos. As we were left alone with our newborn, the room felt sombre, quiet. I felt detached from Saajan but paradoxically also really attached—I *wanted* to take care of him but I felt no connection. Or perhaps I was denying the deep connection that I had felt just hours before as it was veiled by this label?

I recently found a picture of Preetam a few hours after Saajan was born. He was hunched over Saajan's small hospital crib. I now see the sadness in his eyes—they were speaking for his soul. His heart was broken. At that moment, he knew without being told that our worlds were not destined for what we had hoped.

I felt robbed; I had finally experienced bliss and pure joy at the arrival of a newborn—the type that I'd always imagined and yearned for… and it had lasted for all of nine hours.

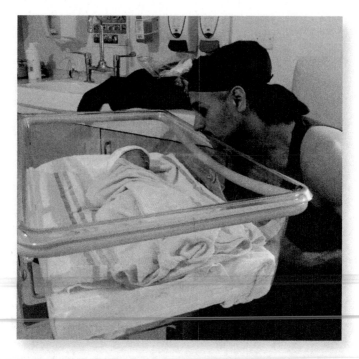

Preetam with Saajan a few hours after he was born

How was I going to share with the world what had "happened"? Our friends? Our blog followers who knew our baby was due any time? How was I going to face everyone? What words would I use? What I did know was that my narrative would influence and dictate how the world accepted him but I wasn't ready to muster up the words, nor did I have the courage to put on a brave face.

My sisters came armed with gifts. I felt the warmth rise from my heavy heart to my head and without warning, tears started streaming. "You still bought gifts even though he has Down's syndrome?" I blurted between sobs, almost searching for reassurance unknown to me at the time. They both burst into tears—"How can you even think we'd love him any less, Harps?"

That night, the nurse took Saajan to draw blood from him to confirm his diagnosis. Preetam went with him and returned to the room 45 minutes later crying—the pain and anguish in his demeanour couldn't go unnoticed. Saajan's blood was so thick that it kept clotting and they struggled so much that they ended up drawing it from his head. Did he have leukaemia? Is that why his blood was clotting? Were we about to face an even bigger battle? I could visibly see the weight on Preetam's shoulders as he struggled to process what was unfolding before our eyes.

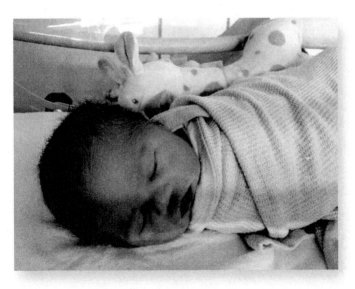

Saajan at a few hours old

I scanned Saajan's face as he lay in his crib oblivious to the chaos that he'd brought with him. While wallowing in self-pity, I felt a wave of sadness for him. Why did this innocent little human have to undergo so much already? He was peaceful and content; he was already different to what I'd embarrassingly assumed a baby with Down's syndrome would be like. Where had my shallow perceptions come from? The room felt eerily silent as Preetam and I were consumed by our own thoughts.

Moments later. the doctor reluctantly came in, "I'm really sorry to inform you—Saajan's blood sugar has dropped and he is struggling to regulate his own body temperature. He will need to be placed in neonatal."

What?

I knew from passing conversations with friends that "neonatal" was the newborn intensive care unit (NICU). I'd never even thought about the chance of my child having to be placed in intensive care! I had no idea what to expect. I felt sick. My stomach began to churn as this new hurdle presented itself. I felt confused. I feared that being physically separated from my baby was going to further create distance between us. Everything felt like it was happening so fast. Was God perhaps giving us new challenges to give us perspective on our reaction to the last? How had so much happened in just the space of a few hours?

Saajan was taken to NICU and placed in an incubator—seeing his swollen little body lying there added to my confusion. I was unable to hold him, to feel him, to smell him. I couldn't get my head around what was happening. I wasn't able to feed him—the one thing that I'd managed to successfully do with him, was robbed of me. He was being tube fed to try and regulate his temperature. Why was he enduring so much already? It felt unfair that he wasn't able to have the comfort of my heartbeat and me his. The looming distance mounted but closed off all at once. I struggled to make sense of it. I felt helpless and devastated at how my new life was unfolding. This wasn't how it was supposed to be.

It was about 9 pm and the staff had managed to settle Saajan in NICU. I felt comforted by the kind and gentle staff. Their tenderness towards Saajan helped. Did I assume that everyone he encountered would mistreat him because of his extra chromosome? Maybe. In those initial moments, I selfishly felt exhausted by the thought of spending the remainder of my life defending my child. I just wanted a "normal" life. Preetam left to go home, escaping to familiarity.

I was left alone in a private room, just me and my thoughts. It felt like the midwives and doctors were almost too fearful to enter not knowing what to say. I welcomed the avoidance over the "I'm so sorry; I know your life is going to be very different from what you imagined." by a few. Each time felt like a punch in my ribs. Why were *they* sorry? I didn't want to hear that. I wanted to hear that everything was going to be okay. I wanted hope. I wanted a silver lining but I couldn't see past the thick fog that consumed me. But I didn't blame them—they were perhaps saying what they felt the right thing was based on my reaction. The midwives felt helpless but I appreciated their kindness.

"Mild Down's syndrome" was the first thing I searched for on Google—desperate to find hope that my child only had "it" mildly. Why did I want him to have it mildly? What did that mean? What was I so afraid of? Where was this sense of entitlement coming from? I very quickly learnt that there was no such thing as "mild" or "severe" Down's syndrome. You either have it or you don't. For example, as is the case with typically developing children, some with Down's syndrome may find it easier to ride a bike than do maths while others may find maths a lot easier than balancing on a bike. People with Down's syndrome all possess different strengths and challenges.

"Is Down's syndrome a disability or a learning difficulty?" was the second thing I googled. Unbeknown to me at the time, I was embarrassingly consumed by the stigma attached to these labels. How had I subconsciously become so biased? My stomach knotted as the reality dawned on me—I *was* a mother to a child with a disability. It was my choice whether I decided to let the label and stigma attached to it define our lives or whether I was going to choose to be that change. Which way was my life heading?

I frantically searched the "Down's syndrome" hashtag on Instagram during my sleepless nights in the hospital, desperate for hope. I was in awe of how devoted many parents were to their children, patiently practising what, up until then, I had considered basic tasks such as learning to stand, holding a pen, or learning a new word. Up until then, I had never valued and appreciated the beauty in growth where it didn't come so easily. Arjun had hit his milestones without many challenges so perhaps we had taken it for granted. Of course, we had celebrated his milestones but it felt so different to witness these children reaching the same milestones.

I remembered that a friend of mine had a friend, Nisha, who had a son with Down's syndrome, Kush. I searched for their page (@T21TeamKush) and one by one went through Nisha's pictures and videos. I was in awe of Kush's ability to sign so fluently—I was amazed by his mother's dedication and patience.

As amazingly as those kids were doing, I didn't want my child to have to work so hard to achieve the things that come naturally to typically developing children. What was *his* future going to look like? I didn't want his life to feel so difficult. I wanted it to be simple for him. What was *our* future going to look like?

Nisha and Kush gave me hope, though, that we could be a relatively "normal" family, albeit a different kind of normal.

I wasn't ever one of those mums who spent hours sitting on the floor playing with her kids, or that had the patience to learn an entirely new language—sign language. I didn't feel good enough to be a special educational needs (SEN) mum. I didn't want to be one because I didn't believe I could be.

Preetam immersed himself in Arjun and found solace in him. I almost felt envious that he had the option to escape where I didn't. I felt trapped. I felt like this was "my problem". I've always referred to Preetam as our real-life Superman, but, for the first time, we were in a situation that he was unable to "fix". He felt helpless. With that feeling of helplessness came a growing distance from those around him which filled me with panic. Did he blame me? Or was it because he was consumed by desperately trying to find a solution? What was he thinking? The emotional pain I felt numbed the physical pain I felt from my surgery as intrusive thoughts consumed me.

The next morning, New Year's Eve, Mané had given birth to a beautiful little boy, Sarvun, in the same hospital. She came up to see me before being discharged. "He has Down's syndrome" I blurted out through sobs. She hugged me. "I know, it's okay. We are going to be okay. You are lucky to be chosen to be his mum. You are a good mum who will be able to look after him so that's why he chose you." Her demeanour was calm and I took so much comfort in her embrace. I recalled a conversation that we'd had whilst pregnant—Mané had mentioned that they'd never terminate their unborn child if they found out he or she had Down's syndrome; I took so much comfort in knowing that. She wasn't speaking empty words; she meant what she said.

I felt devastated that all the plans we'd made together for our maternity leave were probably going to be tainted by the grief we were facing. This wasn't how it was supposed to be. I was gutted. I felt so guilty that the birth of her son was shadowed by what was going on in her brother's life. I didn't want that but I didn't know how to shake it.

That night, Goov stayed with me at the hospital. I woke up in the middle of the night gasping for breath; it took a few moments for me to realise I wasn't dreaming and that in that moment, my reality was the nightmare.

I was a special needs mum.

We had a son with Down's syndrome.

As my sister watched the New Year's fireworks from our window and the world celebrated the turn of a new year, my life was falling apart. Where was life going to take me? What was the fate of my family? Would Preetam hang around? This was truly going to make or break our family.

I was paralysed with fear as we waited for the genetics test results. Was it my fault? Would I be blamed for this?

My feelings were exacerbated by being away from the guy who had always given me strength—my Arjun. He wasn't able to visit NICU which meant he didn't come to the hospital often. He was being kept busy by our family—the novelty of having so many people around him was a good distraction. I was able to pop home a few times during our hospital stay and every time I did, it was like a brief escape. A temporary safety net where I could escape my reality. I remember savouring my mother-in-law's "loon valeh chawl" (spiced rice) with plain yoghurt and feeling the warmth of my life before this ordeal.

I dreaded the time that those moments of escapism drew closer to an end and I had to return to the hospital that had become my prison—the prison that housed my new reality. Our families were at our house daily; my sisters and Indy stayed to support us however they could. No one really knew what to do but they wanted to be with us. I was grateful for the familiarity and comfort of the family. Indy couldn't use his usual charm of making us laugh in this scenario—everyone was processing the news in their own way as they watched their loved ones also trying to process it. Instead, Indy busied himself with washing the dishes and helping with Bruno.

On New Year's Day, we received the results of the blood test.

It was confirmed. Saajan had Trisomy 21.

I grieved even harder as the hope I held on to that perhaps the doctors had got it wrong slipped through my fingers.

There are three types of Down's syndrome:

- **Trisomy 21:** About 95 percent of people with Down's syndrome have Trisomy 21. This is where each cell in the body has three separate copies of chromosome 21 instead of the usual two copies.
- **Translocation Down's syndrome:** This accounts for a small percentage of people with Down's syndrome (about three percent). This is when an extra part or a whole extra chromosome 21 is present, but it is attached or "trans-located" to a different chromosome rather than being a separate chromosome 21.
- **Mosaic Down's syndrome:** This affects about two percent of people with Down's syndrome. For children with mosaic Down's syndrome, some of their cells have three copies of chromosome 21, but other cells

have the typical two copies of chromosome 21. Those with mosaic Down's syndrome may have the same features as others with Down's syndrome. However, they may have fewer features of the condition as some cells have a typical number of chromosomes.

The genetics test confirmed that it was by sheer fluke that Saajan had Trisomy 21.

I reluctantly posted a picture on Instagram of my curly-haired biggest boy beaming from ear to ear holding his new baby brother, pride oozing out of him, silently hinting to the world through my cryptic caption, "Welcome to the world our precious boy... thank you for picking us as your family. This year and forever is about focusing on us as a unit—nothing else matters. Happy New Year x". The *likes* and comments of congratulations poured in as our Instagram family celebrated the arrival of our baby boy, unaware of the heartbreak that was unfolding.

That night, I fell asleep with the comfort of knowing Goov was with me. It was my temporary escape. I woke up from a nap to over 40 messages from friends and family. I was confused about how they knew our son had Down's syndrome.

I pinched myself. Was I having a nightmare? As I woke, startled, I turned to Goov who was still awake, lying on the hospital chair next to me, clearly struggling to fall asleep. "How does everyone know?" I asked as my heart pounded through my chest and my throat closed in as my tears began streaming involuntarily.

"Check the blog."

*The picture of my two beautiful boys
that I posted on Instagram*

I reached back for my phone, and, through watery eyes, typed www.BabyBrainMemoirs.com without question… Unknown to me, Preetam had shared with the world, in a heartfelt post, that our son had Down's syndrome. I read the blog post with my heart racing unable to stop my tears whilst trying to read what was on the screen.

"So, my kid has Down's syndrome. I never really knew what Down's syndrome was, I could easily identify it and tell if someone had Down's syndrome but never understood it.

It's basically a scenario where usually, at the point of conception, the foetus has an extra chromosome (21). Where two chromosomes are expected, you end up with three. In most cases, having one more of something is usually a good thing. However, when it comes to chromosomes, it seems the additional results in slowed learning and a few Down's characteristics.

I am writing this on the evening my second son was born. When he was born, I noticed a few Down's-related features but put it down to him being born at 39 weeks.

Later that evening, a consultant came to see us to confirm that our son does indeed have Down's. The realisation of this broke me. I am not a very humbled or religious person; I am driven and focused but tend not to stop and enjoy let alone being thankful for everything in my life. Deep down, I am thankful in my own way but I don't express this openly. Unfortunately, I can be quite judgemental with little remorse when something frustrates me. I am adamant my son's additional chromosome was indirectly my fault. I didn't intentionally cause it to happen but felt my actions or thought process had led God or the universe to "balance my books". I felt it was a way for him to punish my wrong-doing by punishing my child.

This broke me.

I am far from the perfect husband.

I do, however, try to be a good dad. Prior to Saajan, my second son, I had Arjun. Arjun has been the apple of my eye from the moment he was born. He brought out feelings in me I thought I never had. We are completely besotted with each other and just inseparable. Arjun is perfect. What's funny is I see myself in him every day with his little mannerisms like sticking his tongue out while he is concentrating, or the way he just loves to get involved. I feel I've always known him, maybe connected with his soul in a past life. Some might say our relationship isn't healthy as we both suffer from anxiety when we are initially separated but I wouldn't have it any other way.

So, the thought of something I have done or something I simply haven't done right impacting my child really tore me up. Breaking down randomly, struggling to come to terms with this.

This morning, I went home from the hospital to feed our dog who hasn't been very well. I took her for a walk to clear my head. This is something I've become accustomed to doing for years. There's something about the early morning air, the fog, the crisp breeze that lets you just get lost. I don't meditate, but this time in the morning really lets me just find myself.

I kept questioning why this has happened. Is it because of the way I am? Is it the things I've done that have caused this to happen to my son? Is God punishing me or us? Why is he paying the price?

Harps brought up a funny point that really makes me hate our culture. People just have a habit of talking about "nazar". This is an evil eye; jealousy. Harps doesn't believe in this, and nor do I. I don't believe this exists but the truth is it probably does. That when you have things going right, something will inevitably go wrong. I have everything I could ever wish for. What people don't see is how hard I have to work for it, often sacrificing time with my family. This aside, I have also been a firm believer that problems are opportunities. So even if things go wrong, I'm keen to just take it all in my stride.

I have no doubt I will do my utter best to be a good dad to both my sons. I just can't help but struggle to understand why this might have happened.

I came to the realisation that yes, Saajan has a learning difficulty, but unlike Arjun and I, he will undoubtedly have a much more innocent view on the world. Arjun currently does as he is very young, however, as he gets older and if he follows my traits, he might get a little arrogant in his adolescent years.

My experience of people with Down's syndrome has always been positive, be it seeing children playing or adults offering hugs or smiles to passers-by. Those infrequent experiences give me a very reassuring feeling.

Having a child with Down's, I feel, will be a positive thing. Saajan is a gift. Unlike Arjun and I, he is such a special gift. He has an extra chromosome which makes him very special. He has a head start. He won't feel hate or discrimination. His innocence will last a lifetime.

I always loved seeing the world through Arjun's eyes on holiday, or his appreciation for little things. Not a single day goes by where I don't smile at the things he comes out with. The love he has for his brother melts my heart.

As a family, we can all now see the world through Saajan's eyes. We have been blessed to be able to see the good in everything and really appreciate the world for what it is.

That is something that has been missing from my life. I lack empathy. I don't always see the good. Recently, I feel I have become the first to vent if something isn't done to my satisfaction. But the truth is, not everyone is like you. What you do have are people who are very special, like Saajan, whom I feel I am blessed to father, because, over our lifetimes, I can learn so much from him and become a much better person.

He is a very special soul; Harps thinks he has chosen us to love him and give him the perfect life.

I don't think she is wrong. He truly is a remarkable soul.

Harps is a phenomenal mum; her health has been up and down. She had an emergency C-section again, but straight away, and I have no idea where she has found her strength, she seems completely un-fazed. She is determined to be the best mum to Saajy.

He has a truly amazing big brother. Arjun will certainly keep his little brother on his toes, teaching him to use drills and toy saws! Or the iPad to draw with colours.

More so, he has amazing aunties and uncles. My sisters-in-law are amazing. I love them like my own siblings. Their love for my kids is unconditional; you can see it. The way they drop everything for them, for us. Harvs, Goovy, love you both loads! X And Indy! Thank you for being there. Helping us through our day-to-day.

The truth is, I don't want Harps to go through PND again. I'm not one to talk about my feelings or to share how I feel. I just keep quiet and get on with it. I wrote this so she knows she has everyone behind her including me.

The truth is, I wouldn't have wanted it any other way. This gorgeous little man is going to change our lives for the better.

X"

I was stunned. I had no idea Preetam even knew how to access my blog.

His words broke me; I loathed that he was blaming himself for this. I was shocked at his outpouring of emotion and his bravery in posting something for the world to see. His words made me feel safe. They made me feel as though everything was going to be okay. I knew what a huge deal it was for him to have done this—I've mentioned earlier that he's not much of a communicator. I could feel the cultural influences playing into how he felt—the concept of "nazar" and having a bad omen on you was something familiar to us.

It was about 11 pm. I went straight down to see Saajan in NICU. In that moment, that's all I wanted to do. As I hobbled along the corridor past the window to the room that Saajan was in, I was surprised to see Preetam sitting there holding Saajan, staring at his face. I watched him watching Saajan. I could see how conflicted he felt—society and stigma told us that this was "wrong" but in our hearts, we couldn't help but feel love and protection.

I entered after a few minutes of observing and embraced him as I broke down.

"I want you to know that you're not alone." he said. I suddenly felt weak again. There was something about what he'd just said that made me feel *really* alone. What did he mean? Was this being perceived as my sole responsibility? I felt confused as I felt a weight in my heart. I was left to conjure up my own conclusion.

I felt overwhelmed by the messages I was receiving and the outpouring of love for my son and for our family from complete strangers on the blog. I felt relieved that I wouldn't have to be the one to find the words to tell the world. With the revelation came so many messages from parents of children with Down's syndrome that were further down the road in this journey. People who actually had a valid opinion. People who promised me it would be okay. People who would become my virtual family.

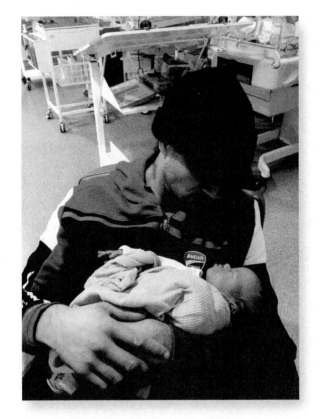

Preetam with Saajan in NICU

"Congratulations, huni! I can't wait to meet him!" read a message from my friend Suky. "He has Down's syndrome", I replied. "I know! I can't wait to see you guys!" she said. I couldn't believe that she was still excited to meet him.

I felt warmth from our family; I felt their sheer desperation in wanting to help; wanting to let us know that they were all there.

"Harps, we're coming to see you!" The words Sav had typed reminded me that we were in this together and that it was going to be okay. "No, don't come", I replied, not wanting to face the world.

Despite my avoidance, Sav still came to the hospital with her fiancé, Jazz. I felt cross with her for coming against my will and refused to see them; I couldn't face anyone. I wasn't the Harps they had once known. I didn't know who I was anymore. The midwife came in to deliver the gifts that they had brought. I broke down seeing the little elephant comforter. It showed me how helpless she felt. Knowing I was in pain was also paining her; how badly she just wanted to be there for me. Where I'd always turned to my friends throughout life's struggles, this struggle didn't feel like it was one that anyone could help me with. I will always remember that gesture, that despite me rejecting her, she still came to show me she was there. She's always been a woman of action!

I had the odd "I'm so sorry" message. "Sorry for what?" I thought. Why would they be sorry? Nothing had "happened" to them. Those words sent me into a frenzied panic. All I needed was to know that my son would be accepted and be loved.

Despite Preetam's outpouring of love and support in his blog post, I felt so lonely. I wasn't able to escape home whenever I wanted and nuzzle into the familiar smell of Arjun's hair and get lost in a world other than my own, even momentarily. Where had the dream of my perfect future escaped to? Life felt so cruel.

3rd January 2017, 7.29 am. I received a WhatsApp message from a number that wasn't saved in my phonebook:

"Hello! My name is Nisha and I'm a friend of Shiv! She told me you just had a baby boy, congratulations!!!! She also told me he is a baby who has Down's syndrome, just like my Kush! I know exactly what you are going through right now, because we went through the same thing when Kush was born, and honestly, hand on heart please don't waste this time worrying, enjoy him!!! Enjoy these early days as you did your first. You won't get them back, and I regret wasting the time at the beginning instead of loving my baby for what he was/is.

Yes, it's scary, it's upsetting to your core and you just don't know WHY this has happened to your boy. But seriously, it's not that bad!! It's not all doom and gloom and it's not parents who haven't been through this perceive, you don't need their pity, because your baby is going to do everything! Yes, it will take longer, and yes you will face challenges, and some days will be much harder than others. But there is so much support out there and so much help/therapy that you can go to to help your little one along when he's is ready. But for now, enjoy him. I'm happy to have a chat with you on the phone or come over etc as we're living proof life will be ok again!! We have a great life enriched all the more by my Kushi. He's changed me and my family for the better and I couldn't go a day in my life without him.

He is just a baby, and for the next 6 months he will do what every baby does… eat, sleep and poop. But know in the back of your mind that this is going to be ok!! I know back then if someone told me all this, I'd struggle to imagine I'd ever feel that way and that life would ever be any better… but it will be. That I promise xxxxx"

I figuratively felt a warm embrace from someone that just "got it". It was the first time I truly felt seen and it was because I was reading these words from someone that had walked this path. Her words weren't loaded with negativity, instead they were quite the opposite! She was encouraging me to enjoy my baby boy—she knew from experience, but I couldn't shake this feeling. I replied:

"Hey Nisha, thank you so much for your message and for taking the time out to provide me with hope.

I've woken up today ready to just give up on life. This isn't how I imagined it to be. This wasn't how it was supposed to be. I'm grieving for a baby I thought I was going to have and I equally feel so guilty when I look at him. I'm struggling to look past his features, everything that's happening I'm associating with Down's. How will I ever ride this journey? I'm one of the weakest people I know. I feel so lonely. I know my husband is riding his own emotions—he's seeking so much comfort in our first born but I'm here at hospital waiting for Saajan to feel better.

How do I know how severe it will be? How do I know he'll be ok in life? He won't be forever dependent on his older brother? How do I know he'll make friends? Won't get bullied?

How am I going to do this?

Please tell me I'll feel better when we are all home together as a family? Please tell me things will be "normal"? Please tell me our lives won't just be filled with hospital appointments?

Seeing your boy gave me so much hope—he is so beautiful and I was so in awe of yours and your husband's dedication to him—he is thriving.

Preetam works Monday—Friday and does his own business outside of that. Am I going to be left alone to do this by myself? What am I going to do when his paternity leave finishes and I feel this way? How will I cope?

I'm so sorry for putting this on you and perhaps taking you back to the initial days but I don't know what to do. I am so drained. Feel numb like I'm in a bad dream. X"

Nisha and I continued to speak and very quickly, she became a huge source of comfort. I could sense the love and excitement from her message for she knew something that I didn't yet know. I could speak the words and feelings I was perhaps too scared to share openly in fear of judgement but also in fear of giving others permission to feel the same as me. I still wanted to protect Saajan. I wanted him to be loved and accepted.

I persevered with breastfeeding for the first three days of Saajan's life as I watched my helpless innocent little human already fighting. By now, I knew why the midwives had commented on him latching on so well when he was born—because apparently, children with Down's syndrome struggle to breastfeed due to low muscle tone. He was already challenging stereotypes!

We learnt that 40 percent of all babies born with Down's syndrome have a heart defect which often requires surgery. Saajan was set to have his echo on the third day of his life. I held my breath praying that all would be okay. Statistics no longer comforted me given we had been the anomaly.

Our scan came back clear.

We were the lucky ones and that became my only source of comfort—that our son hadn't been born with any health problems. We were told we'd receive a follow-up scan in a few months just to be sure but I was comforted by the scan we'd had enough to put it at the back of my mind.

Every time I looked at him, I felt guilty. He'd done nothing. Nothing had happened to him—he was exactly the way he was meant to be. Paradoxically, though, I felt like I was rejecting him, although there was a part of me that wanted to provide for him—I was religiously waking up every two hours during the night to go to NICU to feed the baby. Puffy-eyed, I'd end up in tears every single time I saw him. I felt physically weak from the C-section and mentally weak from all that was going on. I felt the pain of our situation physically too. The NICU nurses were amazing. I didn't even understand my tears. I was so confused by our situation. I wished I could escape and go home and be with Arjun instead. At that time, I'd look at Saajan's innocent little face and cry that I felt like my love for him had conditions attached to it; that a label could turn my love into pain.

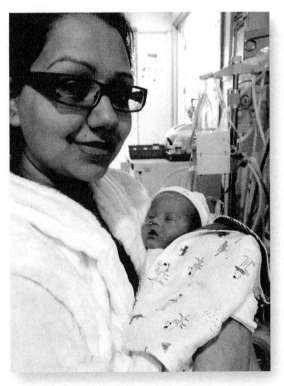

Saajan & I in NICU

Saajan spent five days in NICU, away from me.

I'd been paralysed from the pain the first time I had had a C-section, but this time, I didn't have time to even process my physical pain. It was numbed by my heartache and emotional pain.

Six days later, we were finally allowed home.

CHAPTER 16:

Feeling the Unexpected… Again

"CONGRATULATIONS IT'S A BOY" read the banner hanging from our living-room ceiling. I cried when I saw that my sisters had decorated the house to welcome us home the same way they had when Arjun was born. How could they be acting so normal? This *wasn't* normal. To them, it didn't matter that Saajan had Down's syndrome. Saajan was their little nephew and they saw no difference.

Arjun was ecstatic to have his baby brother home. He sat by him cooing and asking to hold him. He hadn't seen him since the day he was born and his heart was yearning for it. My heart felt full watching them—would Arjun still feel this way when he realised Saajan was "different"?

Our families were all there on our arrival, and it felt comforting to be surrounded by them again. The last time we'd all been together was the day that Saajan was born and the shambolic scene had erupted on sharing the news

The day Saajan came home… our hearts still heavy as we processed the news of our baby having Down's syndrome

of Saajan's diagnosis. It felt like such a long time ago. I was grateful for my sisters—though they probably were hurting for me, they did such a good job at masking any of those emotions and scooping Saajan up and playing with their new nephew.

Both our families were always present; someone was with us every single day for the first three weeks, and my sisters and Indy took it in turns to stay the night with us. It filled the awkwardness that was mounting between Preetam and I. It gave him more of a reason to talk about "it" as little as possible. As each day passed, Preetam became more and more withdrawn. I wanted to talk yet he had nothing to say. I wanted to cry where he was numb

Arjun besotted by his new baby brother

to his tears. I had no idea what was running through his mind but I knew he felt helpless. I was terrified of what our future held. Were we going to make it? Was I going to end up a single mother raising a disabled child by myself? I was so fixated on how he was feeling that I ignored my dark thoughts. My mind was in overdrive clouded by intrusive thoughts and the fear of what our future held. We were both so consumed by grief.

While I was so consumed by all these fears and worries, Arjun felt like the least of my worries—he was easy. He was the only thing in my life that wasn't causing me any stress. He was my relief but I felt so guilty for leaning on him so heavily without really understanding what his needs were. But now—I needed him. He had no

Indy with his new nephew

idea how much comfort I took in his embrace; how much strength I took from his love.

I wish I could have savoured my last few months with Arjun as an only child a lot more than I had. I missed him. I really missed him. I missed him growing up without even realising because I was too preoccupied with my own self-pity.

His nursery key worker mentioned that he'd been relatively quiet and withdrawn at nursery which added to my guilt—he wasn't able to articulate it, but the weight of our worries was weighing heavily on his shoulders.

We were assigned a paediatrician at the Children's Development Centre where we were told that Saajan would receive physiotherapy and speech and language therapy (SALT) when he was old enough. Dr K also explained that there was a really great local charity known as Sparkles—a charity I'd heard of from Nisha, Kush's mother. I'd seen the difference Sparkles had made to Kush and I knew that although at that time, I didn't want to be surrounded by people with Down's syndrome, it was the right thing to do for my child.

Saajan at his first physiotherapy session with the NHS

We were inundated with appointments for the ears, eyes, heart and thyroid. I didn't want to have a diary dedicated just to appointment management. I hated visiting the hospital, seeing the maternity unit and so badly wanting to go back to being blissfully ignorant in pregnancy.

I very clearly remember the first time we visited the Children's Development Centre and saw a child with Down's syndrome who was about three and unable to hold his neck up. I felt suffocated and tears began streaming down my face before I was sobbing uncontrollably and ran out of the room almost gasping for air. How would I take care of Saajan?

Arjun had to get used to a new normal—one where we would often attend hospital appointments. One where he'd be surrounded by doctors and nurses. He managed it so gracefully. But I was hurting for him.

I'd look outside into our garden—the beautiful bifold doors we'd carefully selected while I was pregnant, the marble worktops, the bouncy carpet—none of it mattered anymore. It would house a disabled child.

How would we ever go on holiday with him? How would he ever fly? "He'll hate the sand and people," I thought.

Every day was a battle. Every day I'd wake up and wonder how this was reality. I'd wonder how I could end this "nightmare"? I had the darkest thoughts I've ever experienced—so many of which I'm so ashamed of now. Adoption? Preetam was repulsed by this suggestion— though it felt like he too was rejecting Saajan at the time,

*The bifold doors that I'd often look out
of and ponder over our future*

his fierce protective father side came out immediately after my suggestion. Did I think we could magically just go back in time? Our family would never be the same again, Arjun would be heartbroken. Preetam and I wouldn't last. What if *I* ended it all? I'd be free from the worry, the guilt, the devastation; but how selfish would that be? Where would that leave Arjun and Saajan? The thought of ending it all crossed my mind more than any of the other options—it felt like the least devastating option and the one that felt easiest, or so I thought. Perhaps having another baby straight away would help?... Despite how I was feeling, looking in to Saajan's pure eyes whilst having such thoughts was enough to make me loathe myself—he was innocent, full of love and I knew deep down that adoption wouldn't solve the deep grief I was feeling.

Slowly, I began to realise there was no solution other than to face our new reality.

Every day, I'd fear for our future—for my marriage, for my family, for my coping skills. I'd worry about how we'd be treated at the Gurdwara—so much so that we didn't go very often in the beginning. It was my dad who reminded me of Guru Nanak Dev Ji's first teaching—we are all God's children and that we are all equal regardless

Saajan & his Nana Ji

of race, gender, age or ability. Saajan has as much of a right to be at the Gurdwara as anyone else. Every day, I'd wonder if he'd even be loved by others like Arjun was. Every day that I spent doing this was a day I missed out on Saajan and Arjun growing up. Hours merged into days, days into weeks, and weeks into months as I struggled to shift the black cloud that was looming over me. I remember so little of Saajan's first year. Even his milestones and when they were achieved are a blur.

There would be days when I was alone with the kids and sadness would strike so deep that I would question my ability to be their mother as I wallowed in self-pity. My sister Goov would call on her lunch break, as she did religiously, and there were times I'd break down—times when I didn't know how to save face; when I just wanted it all to be over. She'd leave work to come to see me. I was so grateful to her manager for allowing her to be there for me and for the compassion that complete strangers showed to our situation. I remember her coming over in response to my hysteria. As I tearfully shared some of my dark thoughts with her, she burst out crying, not because she felt sad for me but because she felt so heartbroken over what I was saying. "How can you write him off before you've even given him a chance?" she asked.

Everywhere I went, I'd see new mums floating on cloud nine with joy from their new babies. I remember Preetam suggesting a family day out to Ashridge—a gorgeous National Trust Park. I was excited to just be a "normal family", but my emerging excitement quickly turned to heartache as a group of NCT mums sat down

Arjun & Saajan with their Goov masi

at the table next to us with their perfect newborn babies, loudly chatting away excitedly about the sleepless nights and the magical moments. My life felt bleak; I *had* to care for Saajan; it didn't feel like it was a choice. It didn't feel exciting.

I struggled to be around other children especially around the same age as Saajan while I dealt with my own

Arjun & Saajan with their Harv masi

grief. I felt selfish. I couldn't help but focus on how much they were achieving while my son's development was at a standstill. I was aware of my lack of attention towards Saajan as I was fixated on torturing myself with the gap that existed at such a tender age between him and his peers. I just couldn't help myself. As for the milestones that felt had come quite quickly with Arjun, such as first smiles, we felt like we were waiting forever with Saajan. I had no motivation to focus on my child, but I felt immense love for him when I *did* pay attention.

I'd look at myself in the mirror with my hair looking limp, dark circles under my swollen eyes—our eyes are definitely a window to our souls. My soul was hurting. Who had I become? I was unrecognisable. I used to wonder if I'd ever wear make-up again, if I'd ever care about the clothes I was wearing again, if I'd ever don my big hair again—you can spot me from a mile just from my big hair. All of those felt like a big part of me. I liked looking nice. I let that go.

My face and appearance reflected my feelings.

Gloomy.

Dark.

Heartbroken.

Sad.

Where my employer was so compassionate and wanted so desperately to help the situation, Preetam's employer had a less sensitive approach. We were processing the enormity of our reality while having to manage the day-to-day struggles with his employer over something that felt so trivial—support and approved time off to attend appointments. While we were trying to come to terms with an unexpected diagnosis, Preetam's employer refused to give him time off to attend initial appointments and instead, he was forced to use annual leave—leave that was so precious to our family time. It may seem trivial to some, but it felt like a double blow. Through our experience, I've learnt the importance of empathy and compassion and how much of a difference they can make to any situation.

Though my boss was beyond supportive, I feared how I'd ever return to work or how I'd face everyone. How could I take my disabled baby to meet everyone on a 'keeping in touch' day? What would our GP say? What about the pharmacy and local shopkeepers? What would everyone think? How would he be treated?

Friends and extended family constantly reached out to us, some saying the right things, some, unbeknown to them, sending me into an even deeper hole. I gauged people's reactions from their words. I took comfort in those who congratulated us and told us they couldn't wait to see us. I felt comforted that they didn't seem to care that he had an extra copy of chromosome 21. I felt like those who said, "I'm sorry," were really saying, "Thank God it's not us". I took very little comfort in talking to friends or family who hadn't been through this—it felt like everyone was just relieved that it wasn't "happening" to them. This was our reality.

I barely responded to people. I didn't want to see anyone other than our immediate family. I didn't want to speak to anyone. I had nothing to say. No one could change my fate. The only place I visited in the first few months of Saajan's life was my in-laws' house and sometimes my parents' house. My in-laws' home very quickly became my safe haven. Though they were as shocked by the news of Saajan's diagnosis as we were, their focus very quickly turned to loving Saajan deeply. On the days when I struggled to take care of myself let alone Saajan, my in-laws stepped in. From as early as two weeks old, Saajan began staying the night at my in-laws' when I didn't feel as though I could cope.

Saajan & his Dadi Ji

Though their house became my safe haven, I often struggled with my mother-in-law leaning on me as her shoulder to cry on. I had no idea how to respond. Some days, I would go over feeling like I was okay and I would quickly be knocked back by an innocent comment about how she may have been feeling down about the diagnosis and why. I wasn't strong enough at that time to be able to support others. But I knew that my mother-in-law had a deep love for Saajan and that kept me patient. I could see behind their brave faces that they were also struggling.

My father-in-law's love and devotion to Saajan is crystal clear to see. Saajan's Dada Ji would lovingly massage his little limbs to get him stronger and to encourage blood flow, he'd feed him with so much patience and take care of him with so much love. Not a lot has changed even today!

Saajan & his Dada Ji—a bond like no other

I remember hearing, "He doesn't look like he has Down's syndrome" from many people and feeling relieved. Almost doing a happy dance in my head. I'm not sure why. What did I think that meant? That he *didn't* have

Down's syndrome? That he looked "normal"? I think it felt like I could momentarily escape from the reality.

Sav would check in on me daily, whether I replied to her or not. She missed the absence of our daily phone calls which we'd been accustomed to for years. I just couldn't bear to speak to anyone. On the odd occasion when I did open up and share my fears and my worries, she'd always responded with "We will deal with this, Harps; he is OURS", never "you" or "yours", always "we" or "ours". Her choice of language made all the difference—I didn't feel so alone.

As each day passed, I felt a burning desire to end it all.

I took solace in Amrit; I knew I had a safe space to be open and honest with no judgement. Amrit would check in on me daily, taking time and patience to let me know that she was there and she was ready as soon as I was ready to see her.

But it still felt like everyone else was outside looking in. No one understood how it felt to be me.

Once we'd been home for a few weeks, I allowed one friend to come over hoping that she'd be able to reassure me as one of her close friends has an older son with Down's syndrome. She'd had a baby a month earlier and as Saajan lay there, she sat on the floor propped up on the sofa right next to him, she asked, "So, did you not have the harmony test done?".

"We had no reason to," I replied.

"We did, and if it had come back positive, we would've terminated." I was mortified. Though it felt like I was rejecting Saajan at the time, I couldn't believe someone could be so cruel to insinuate that my son wasn't worthy of life as he lay there, a foot away from her, innocently sound asleep. How dare she? It felt like a slap across my face. I wanted to tell her to leave my house immediately but I didn't have the strength to. I was already in a dark place. I had taken a leap of faith by allowing someone to come and visit me and it felt like the purpose of her trip was to rub it in my face that her son was born "perfect". I was stunned by her words and what they really meant— that my son wasn't worthy of life in her eyes. Though I felt devastated by the encounter, I was surprised by the burning desire I had to protect my son despite not vocalising it—something I regret to this day. It made me realise I did love him somewhere deep down. He IS worthy of life.

Friends and family who had shown Saajan love, sometimes shared that they'd "do the test"—I let my own imagination conclude whatever that meant. When it came to discussions of screening, to be quite frank, I still wouldn't have it in my heart to listen to news of potential termination from those close to me—I take it incredibly personally and, rightly or wrongly, it's the truth. It's far too close to home.

There was a very clear incident when a family member messaged me and said, "What test did you have done?" "The usual nuchal," I replied. "Oh, okay, because I've asked my husband if we can do extra tests because of what happened to Saajan." OUCH. "What exactly *happened* to Saajan?" I replied. I received a very nervous response. That felt like a knife to my heart. How can people be so insensitive? Just because I've shared some of my heartache, that doesn't give people permission to think it's okay to come and talk freely about my child like he is undeserving of life.

We had to return to the hospital for a routine check-up. My stomach was in knots as we pulled up to the familiar tall building of the maternity wing. I felt sick walking back in there—the building that had housed so many memories over the year—both happy and sad, but more recently, sad. As I sat down in the corridor to wait to see the midwife, suddenly, familiar faces started appearing; midwives that I recognised and midwives that I didn't. Before I knew it, there was a queue of hospital staff waiting to give us their congratulations as I sobbed. I recognised the awkwardness they felt not knowing what to say or what to do. I felt so humbled by their love and care. Somehow, everyone within the ward seemed to know what had "happened" to us.

Ms G came to see us. "I have no idea how this was missed but what I do know is—your chances of having him were similar to winning the lottery—he is your jackpot!"—and those words offered me an alternative perspective. It's true—the chance was so low and we were it.

I couldn't stand the sight of the maternity unit. I wished I could be pregnant again like all those other women there—to be back to where I felt happy looking into our future and it looking perfect like those mums at the park. I didn't want this to be my future. I robotically carried on each day on autopilot with no feeling. The continuous visits from the health visitors to make sure I was okay grated on me—I hated everyone because they just didn't get it, they didn't *need* to get it. I felt patronised.

I had no desire to take pictures, and the ones I did, I tried to select carefully—ones that didn't show off his Down's syndrome features. His protruding tongue due to his low muscle tone was my biggest bugbear. I had no desire to use his milestone cards that I'd had custom-made. I forced myself to take monthly pictures—something I was later grateful for.

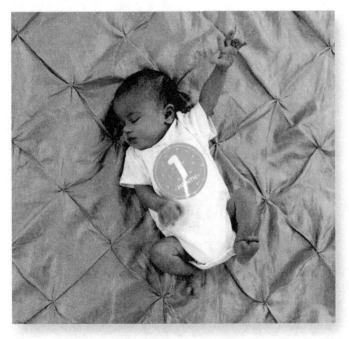

Saajan at one month

People say Saajan had chosen us because we were strong enough; but what if at the time, I didn't want to be chosen? And what choice did we have but to just get on with it? If he had chosen anyone, it felt like Saajan had chosen *Arjun* as his brother more than us as his parents.

Every day, Preetam and I would have *The Secret* playing in the background to stop our minds from

Snoozy snuggles

being consumed by negative thoughts, but the moment it stopped, they'd come flooding back. Though we were coping and processing the news so differently, Preetam and I balanced each other out—when I was consumed by devastation and fearful thoughts about the future, he'd be my strength and vice versa. Though it had felt like the fate of our marriage was unknown because of this, slowly, it became apparent that all we had was each other. Only WE understood OUR situation and OUR pain. Our qualms weren't with each other; they arose out of fear.

CHAPTER 17:

Torn

I HAD COUNSELLING A FEW MONTHS after Saajan was born. I pinned all my hopes on it. I wanted to believe it would "fix" me, that it would be my solution.

It wasn't.

It was the same "your life isn't going to be the same" message being echoed. Why the hell were people telling me this? If I thought about it logically, my life was going okay so far bar a few extra appointments. During the brief moments when I did feel okay, it felt like I was shot down by a comment from a professional telling me that my life wasn't going to be the same and that they were really sorry. It was a sharp pang to my heart each time I heard it and would send me back into my dark hole. It confused me. I almost felt like I was holding my breath anticipating the moment when my life would suddenly be horrendous. I didn't want to keep hearing it, plus, what did they know?! They don't have a child with Down's syndrome.

I considered hypnotherapy to just switch that part of my brain off. I was so desperate for it to all just go away.

I tried anti-depressants—they made me feel alienated. I was in the room, but I wasn't in the room. I decided they weren't for me. I wasn't able to feel, I felt numb but the tablets didn't make my situation disappear.

During this time, my parents were one of my greatest sources of strength—they never cried in front of me other than the day they met Saajan at the hospital when we were hit with the shocking news. They stood tall and celebrated Saajan the same way they celebrated Arjun. They handed out Indian sweets when sharing that they had a new grandson and proudly told the world their grandson had Down's syndrome. That was something that normalised the situation for me—something that gave me hope. If they were okay, I'd be okay. I knew my maternal family would have had their talks amongst themselves but they never let me know of any fears they had. I appreciated that so much as I needed that strength—a strength I've taken from my parents since childhood. They had prayers recited for us all around the world. "Mum, what exactly are you praying for? You know there isn't a cure for Down's syndrome? It's not an illness," I questioned, fearing that the stigma of having a disabled child would be overriding any rationality. "That he has a happy and healthy life," she replied. Phew.

I very vividly remember the feeling of an outpouring of love, as if I was being embraced by warmth from every angle, whenever I spoke to my mum's sisters—they'd check in on me often. They stood tall by us and they

Saajan & his Nani Ji

had an instant love for Saajan, a protectiveness. They'd tell me they were praying for us, for Saajan. They never questioned why—simply embraced Saajan. They didn't care that he had Down's syndrome. He was one of us and that's all that mattered they told me.

My in-laws and their physical support kept me going by offering me a respite to process my life, to give me some breathing space.

We were assigned a key worker, Sian, by the Local Authority. I felt apprehensive about meeting Sian; would she be like the health visitors and counsellor? Would I feel patronised?

Her demeanour was warm and friendly. It was clear she had a love for her job—that precious task of picking up heartbroken families and letting them know it was going to be okay and being there to assist in the logistical and practical side of things. Before Sian, I felt lonely. Though no one said it, it felt like I was expected to remember everything as I was thrown into this whirlwind. I felt scared; overwhelmed. I naturally took a lead on diary management as Preetam led on holding us together for appointments. Sian was there to help with the simplest of tasks, from obtaining helpful information to chasing up appointments, to just listening to me. She would visit every so often and I knew she was only a call or text away. I felt less alone and less overwhelmed.

The doctors, health visitor and Sian had recommended several support groups that were available for us to attend, to meet other parents in our position, but neither Preetam nor I felt it was the right thing for us so early on. We didn't want our entire life to become consumed by this one thing. I didn't want all of our friends to only be parents of those with Down's syndrome. Neither of us wanted that. I wanted our life to be "normal".

The more time that lapsed, the more families I connected with on social media—BabyBrainMemoirs. com suddenly became a lot bigger than what I ever could have imagined. It was now my access to other families, to a network, without feeling overwhelmed and consumed by Down's syndrome. It became a form of therapy. I was able to dip in and out of social media without having to physically see anyone—it felt comfortable and safe. I had several mothers who contacted me who had also received an unexpected diagnosis around the same time as us. We ploughed through our grief together. We understood each other without speaking any words. It was calming to know I wasn't alone; we weren't alone.

I began to connect with families who had such uplifting and inspiring stories—ones where the families DID have a choice, and they CHOSE to proceed with their pregnancies or stories where the family chose to adopt a child with Down's syndrome.

When I first stumbled upon Kelsi's Instagram page, @ DownRightWonderful, I was in absolute awe. I found the family's story so compelling. It's a unique and beautiful story—one of pure love. After the birth of their fifth child, Colt, who was diagnosed with Down's syndrome shortly after his birth, they found his little something extra was wonderful, and he changed their lives and hearts forever leading to the adoption of their sixth child, Nic, who also happens to have an extra chromosome. For me, it was a game changer—not only did they accept Colt so gracefully, but they also went on to make a choice of having another child with Down's syndrome. Someone out there wanted a child like mine. That was what I needed to see—someone WANTED a child like MINE. I'd spend any stolen moments watching Kelsi's Insta stories to see all six of her children running free on their farm—not a worry in the world. They rejoice in the beauty that Down's syndrome has brought them. I wanted to be like them. I wanted the same for my family. They made my heart sing. Watching them interact with their family and with each other was so heart-warming. Kelsi and her husband's faith in God was something that resonated with me—but they celebrated unconditionally where I struggled.

Jai was someone who would sometimes reply to my Insta stories even before I had Saajan. She'd reached out to me to offer words of comfort during those initial low days of motherhood after I'd just had Arjun... What I didn't know at the time was what a dark journey she'd been through herself. She'd devastatingly lost her beautiful daughter, Jazmine, while pregnant. Jazmine was a twin. Every time I have a low moment, I'd think of Jai and her courage, I think of Jazmine, her beautiful angel baby who happened to have Down's syndrome, and I am automatically uplifted. Jai's grief was so poignant. I felt selfish at times when I felt low—Jai so desperately wanted to be with Jazmine, to hold her, to smell her. She'd known her daughter may have Down's syndrome and it hadn't changed her desire to want to keep her. Jai did a skydive for Jazmine and her twin, Jian-Jazmine on their birthday so she could be closer to Jazmine in heaven. The more Jai and I spoke, the more my heart grew for Saajan. Her time and desire to help me, even while going through her own turmoil, meant that I knew what a rare kind she is and it felt good knowing we could help each other.

Kamaljit and Sarbjit both reached out to me—both have sons with Down's syndrome. I took great comfort in them because they had the same faith in God as I did. Being the same religion and understanding the nature of going to the Gurdwara, and the anxieties I had around this, was also a great comfort.

I remember receiving a message from Amber on Instagram that asked something like, "Are you from the UK??!" I will never forget her pure excitement when she found out I was! Amber is a vivacious little firecracker with a heart of gold. She sees no difference and is probably one of the biggest Down's syndrome advocates I've ever encountered. Amber has no direct relation to anyone with Down's syndrome. From a really young age, she had decided that she'd be dedicating her life to supporting those with Down's syndrome. Apart from being a support worker, she has many close friends who have Down's syndrome. She goes on nights out and on shopping sprees with them, and she says that her life would not be the same without them. Her best friend, Claire, would sometimes send me video messages—her zest for life and bright personality would instantly put a smile on my face!

Any time I had a question such as, "Can people with Down's syndrome use a kettle?" or "Can people with Down's syndrome be left home alone?", I'd go straight to Amber. Her network and direct experience meant that she'd always be able to give me an open and honest answer and generally, the answers always instilled me with hope. Amber always shared how inspired she was by her friends with Down's syndrome and that most of her friends could do things that she's still unable to do, such as using a washing machine! Haha!

She always reminded me that based on her experience, many adults with Down's syndrome were a reflection of their upbringing but, of course, every individual is different. It's something I always remember while bringing up Saajan—like any child, I have expectations of him the same way that I do Arjun.

Amber has a pure heart of gold and what I wish for is a world full of people with as pure a lens as she has.

Another account I loved following was Sarah's (@DontBeSorry2). Her son Oscar happens to have Down's syndrome and their family reminded me so much of mine—Chris, her husband, was so similar to Preetam, a handyman, fitness fanatic and a big kid. She has two other children younger than Oscar. I remember very clearly one day, I was watching her Instagram stories and saw Oscar helping Chris lay down breeze blocks for their extension—I felt like it was something I could connect with because that's exactly how Arjun was with Preetam and how we'd always imagined our second child would be. When Saajan was born, I assumed he'd be a forever baby and that none of our hopes or dreams would materialise. Watching Oscar so beautifully getting involved, just like his siblings, filled me with so much hope. I felt excited. I showed Preetam the clip and I saw a glimmer of hope in his eyes too.

I wondered if I'd ever blog again; that fire had died along with the perfect child that I thought I was going to have. Would I ever be in the place that the mums who were helping me are in? I was often told, "Harps, you'll be helping others one day, in a greater way than you ever could have imagined", but I didn't want to help people anymore.

I was done being the strong one. I just wanted a normal simple life. "Special kids are born to special parents"—it felt so patronising. I know people meant well, but it just felt so cliché, and condescending. I'm not special. I always questioned my ability as a mother to a typically developing child. How the hell was I cut out for this?

Would I ever be able to embrace our fate? I had to some extent accepted it because of my faith but I couldn't see the light; all I could see was a thick black fog clouding everything. Nisha reassured me and promised me that I wouldn't feel like this forever and that it would be okay. I trusted her. Writing and sharing my thoughts on the blog used to be my therapy but even that felt futile—how would that help me? How would that solve any of my worries? I often contemplated packing the blog in and shying away from what sometimes felt like a false pretence. I didn't want the world to know how deeply I was grieving. I wanted the world to love my son and, in every blog post I wrote, I tried to ensure I was portraying that as well as my hurt. I was careful not to give people permission to feel what I was. I wanted acceptance. I wanted reassurance. I wanted to know it was going to be okay.

Preetam was so hands-on with Saajan's appointments —more so than I was. He took the lead in attending them. Over time, we began to use hospital appointments as an excuse to spend time as a family. We'd incorporate brunch or lunch with an appointment so that the entire focus wasn't on being at the hospital. It didn't feel so heavy. I began to look forward to the family times. They felt less and less daunting. Knowing he was by my side in this

Me and my boys

felt so comforting. I wasn't as alone as I sometimes felt. As each day passed, we grew closer through our children, through our shared love. The child that I thought had broken us, was actually what bought us back together.

During the storm, we had an army of support. The nursery staff at Arjun's nursery were so kind. I'd often break down when dropping Arjun when they asked, "How are you, Harps?" They reassured me that from their

Arjun always showering Saajan with unconditional love

experience of working with children, all would be okay. They went over and beyond to ensure Arjun was okay, to ensure we were okay. They became like an extended family. I was so grateful.

I continued to gauge the reactions of others in my own quest to seek acceptance.

Watching Arjun innocently love his brother was a big lesson for us. He became our teacher. He held no prejudice or judgement towards his brother; he loved him unconditionally. If anything, he was very protective from the get-go—almost intuitively knowing he needed to be. He wasn't constantly scanning Saajan's face to pick out his Down's features like I was—no, he was too busy cooing over his adorable button nose and his soft lips.

CHAPTER 18:

Don't Break My Heart

As TIME WENT ON, PREETAM AND I realised that we were in this together. No one could ever understand better the path we were walking, than us. We took comfort in each other. We went through the motions of rejection, anger, anguish, grief and denial. Any time I had a moment of weakness, Preetam's strength carried me through and vice versa. I value so much the differences that we possess. I've realised the importance of feeling every single emotion—the more I fought them, the stronger they came. I learnt to ride the emotions, to acknowledge them and then put them to the side. I knew that it was futile trying to figure out the "why" to everything. The truth is, we will never know why Saajan was gifted to us—we could spend our whole lives asking the question, but it's a waste of time and we both came to realise that quite quickly.

Some days I would feel like I was closer to accepting the news—or was I just in denial about the future?

Preetam and I began going on weekly date nights—it gave us the opportunity to reconnect and go back to us, to laugh and cry together away from our day-to-day lives. My in-laws would lovingly take care of the boys to facilitate that. He'd wine (alcohol-free!) and dine me in Central London. It became the highlight of my week—to escape with him. Our marriage was injected with newness, excitement and passion. We became closer than ever and more in love than I could have imagined just months before.

Previously, I'd never gone for a motorbike ride with Preetam. I knew that was his stress release and decided it was time for me to try something new. Where before, I'd be terrified of dying, Saajan's birth ignited a "you only live once" attitude in me. Preetam began to take me on long bike rides—it felt nice to be physically close to him as well as to share something that I knew meant a lot to him.

Four months on and we were finally coming to terms with his diagnosis and it felt like we were in a slightly better place. We'd booked our first family holiday as four to Punta Cana, and it was going to be a chance for us to bond and leave his diagnosis at home. We were looking forward and doing things like a "normal" family. Things were good; they were getting better. It was mid-April and I don't remember the date exactly—but it was a hot day. A really hot day. Things felt nice and like they were settling. I felt happy. I felt hopeful.

Saajan, Preetam and I had just been for a pub garden lunch after I'd had a therapy session in Aylesbury. We

One of mine and Preetam's many date nights

headed to our follow-up echo appointment which had been unexpectedly cancelled on arrival a month earlier. We excitedly chatted about Punta Cana and how once we got home from the appointment, we'd get down the suitcases from the attic to start packing.

We entered the hospital oblivious to what was about to unfold. As we entered the doctor's room, I felt a wave of panic but quickly calmed myself down. It was going to be fine. We've had our full dose of what tough times life had to throw at us. It was done. Everything was going to be okay from now on. I didn't feel anxious or nervous as I had great comfort in knowing his initial echo showed no cause for concern.

As soon as Saajan sat down and Dr F placed the probe on Saajan's chest, the colour drained away from the doctor's face—"I don't understand why it's taken so long for this baby to be on my table… He has an AVSD."

A what?!

"So, what does that mean? Will it fix itself?"

"I'm afraid he's going to need open-heart surgery imminently."

I began zoning out—it felt like the room was beginning to close in on me. I felt like the sound of the doctor explaining, Preetam questioning and Saajan cooing and giggling whilst playing with the probe wire started to become fuzzy and distant.

How could this be happening to us? Where was my comfort now that I had a son with Down's syndrome *and* one who would require one of the biggest surgeries possible—open heart surgery? I felt sick. It felt like an out-of-body experience. You hear about other people going through things like this—how were we now one of those people? But at the same time, why not us?

Withdrawn.

Numb.

Shocked.

A mixture of silent tears and blankness. I couldn't even speak. Preetam asked all the questions—to this day, I still don't fully know the technicalities of what Saajan's heart make-up is. They explained what the defect was— Atrioventricular septal defects (AVSD) are a relatively common family of congenital heart defects. They account for about five percent of all congenital heart disease cases and are most common in infants with Down's syndrome.

I was devastated—it was our silver lining that Saajan had no health complications—the line I'd used to comfort Preetam. I felt angry. I could feel my heart beating outside of my chest.

Was this a sick joke?

I never in a million years could have imagined that we'd be faced with this when we got married or fell pregnant.

In my shell-shocked state, I wasn't able to process anything that was going on around me. The words were just noise. Preetam asked when the surgery would be, assuming we were talking months away. No. It would be imminently and within the next month. What about our holiday? The holiday that was meant to give us the time we needed together as a family? The holiday that had so much hope attached to it?

There would be no holiday.

We went from planning on packing for a holiday to packing for the hospital. My heart was breaking. It felt like a weird twist of fate. It was all made worse by the fact that Saajan was in such a good mood, oblivious to what was coming his way. He has the most peaceful soul and takes life in his stride.

We shared the news with our family who were all devastated but reminded us that it was for *his* benefit. I knew all of this. I just selfishly didn't want to go through it all. I was worried about how it would impact on us as a family going through something so heart-breaking— what if he died? There was a 10 percent chance of that happening we were told. That was a higher chance than us having a child with Down's syndrome, and that happened. I was worried about the emotional and mental impact it would have on Arjun—he had become so attached to Saajan. He'd been through so much already with us living away from home for months before Saajan's arrival and I saw what that did to him and how long it took us to work on that. I was sad that we wouldn't be going on holiday. I felt so cheated.

For some horrible reason, it felt like I was thinking about everyone and everything else other than Saajan and the surgery. Perhaps it was because I knew it wasn't within my control, or perhaps I was in denial.

My coping strategy became an avoidance one. Preetam and I dealt with it in the same way. We immersed ourselves in other things. I threw myself into planning Arjun's third birthday—which was scheduled for after Saajan's operation. It was something I had control of. We spent lots of time together as a family—lots of seaside trips, family movie time and BBQs in the build-up to surgery. I tried to put the surgery to the back of my mind, as did Preetam. But there were days we'd wake up having hardly slept—the idea of him being put to sleep didn't sit right with either of us.

My guilt kicked in massively with Arjun because I knew my attention would be unevenly divided when Saajan was in hospital. His nursery key worker had also mentioned that he was missing me in general so I started doing things with him one-to-one once a week—we visited Chessington World of Adventures and had so much fun, we went to soft play or went shopping. All the things I always feared, I suddenly had an urge to do. Things that I would never have imagined doing alone, we did.

Arjun & I out on a mummy and son day at Chessington World of Adventures

Surgery was scheduled for Saturday 26th May but Saajan developed a horrible cough which lasted three weeks—he stopped coughing literally the day before surgery was scheduled.

As desperate as I was to get it over and done with, after a discussion with the surgeon, Mr Michielon, we agreed it would be best to hold fire and it was rescheduled for 6th June. My frustration grew. The more I wanted to carry on with life, the more challenges presented themselves.

May 26th worked so well with Preetam's work commitments, my sister's engagement ceremony (24th June) and Arjun's third birthday (26th June). June 6th really felt like we were cutting it fine. It wasn't that Saajan wasn't a priority. No. Not at all. It was more that I wanted everyone to be able to enjoy their happy moments without them being tarnished by something going wrong. I asked about delaying surgery by a few weeks at least so that we could celebrate Arjun's birthday together as a family but Mr Michielon didn't recommend that. That took away any other worries I had. It sounds pretty selfish, but I felt so torn—I wanted this to have a minimal impact on Arjun too. He'd been so excited about his Paw Patrol party for months and I didn't want anything to change. He'd also been through enough. I obviously wanted Saajan to be okay but, for some reason, I kept deflecting from the surgery.

It was strange. I'm usually a talker but I just couldn't find the words and nor did I feel I wanted to speak about it. I wanted to block it out. I didn't google his condition; I didn't want to know every single detail about the operation as I knew no good would come out of knowing. I left that worry to the surgeon and his team. Mr Michielon instilled me with so much confidence when I spoke to him. My behaviour was odd. Almost unrecognisable. I just prayed.

Where you have nothing else, you have prayers.

My faith and my belief in God are, and always will be, my salvation. I trust every single decision He makes even when I've been mad at some of them.

Sarah had been through the same thing five years earlier with her son Oscar. She prepared me for what to expect. It made a really huge difference to my expectations and the way I managed things. Of course, the outcome of the surgery was unknown but the process of it felt a bit clearer.

CHAPTER 19:

The Morning before the Day After

THE DAY BEFORE WE WERE due to be admitted, I packed our bags and it still didn't feel real. Preetam and I often spoke about how everything felt really surreal. We spent the evening snuggled up in bed as a family, me trying desperately hard not to torture myself by thinking that this could be the last time we were sat here like this as a four. I've always had a habit of mentally torturing myself with morbid thoughts.

Although the Royal Brompton offers accommodation for families of patients in the paediatric intensive care unit (PICU) across the road from the hospital, we decided to turn the experience on its head for Arjun's sake and Preetam suggested we book a hotel for the week so that he, Arjun and I could stay together and make it a little bit like a holiday for Arjun so he wouldn't feel it as much. We booked The Rembrandt in South Kensington.

On the day we were due to be admitted, I spent the morning going into town with Arjun to return a few things. I made lists for his party and contacted suppliers. I found my behaviour really odd and tried to fight it. But I couldn't. So, I let it ride. That's one thing this journey has taught me—be kind to yourself and ride your emotions.

I don't know why I didn't spend all morning with Saajan. Was it because I was scared of getting too attached? I don't know. It wasn't conscious, though.

We received a phone call at 3 pm to say they had a bed available and to come in by 5 pm. I knew this didn't guarantee the surgery would take place but I was hopeful.

We loaded the car and grabbed a late lunch on the way to the hospital. It felt different to driving to our local hospital. It felt nicer. A bit brighter. I really can't explain it. I felt calm and trusting of the professionals. It's the world's second-best hospital for the heart and lungs. How lucky was I that my son would be operated on and taken care of there?

We arrived at the hospital and were greeted by a lovely friendly nurse called Emma. As she took Saajan's observations so lovingly, she told me her brother had Down's syndrome—it made me feel like she "got it" a little. She was so kind and gentle with Saajan.

Preetam went with Saajan to have his bloods drawn. I waited patiently for what felt like forever—it brought back memories of when he was born and they'd tried to draw blood to confirm his diagnosis. He came back about 45 minutes later, visibly very upset. They had tried to draw bloods from his head four or five times unsuccessfully. I felt helpless and I struggled to fight back my tears. If we couldn't handle seeing Saajan in pain from them trying to draw bloods, how would we face the next day?!

Preetam and I bathed Saajan. I couldn't help but wonder if this would be the last ever bath we'd be giving him as I felt a pang in my chest and tears gently rolling down my cheeks.

The anaesthetist came to see us that evening and explain a few bits. I tried to avoid the risk factors as I knew I'd become obsessed. I wanted to think positively or just not think at all.

I stayed with Saajan that night on the ward. I felt grateful that this time, I could sleep by his side unlike our stay in hospital when he was born. His surgery was scheduled for 8 am the next morning. Preetam and Arjun left about 10 pm and checked in at the hotel. My sisters stayed with them at the hotel. Their support, as always, was immeasurable.

Saajan and I had a good night—he slept till the early hours but was nil by mouth from 2 am. He was allowed water up until 6 am. I'd never given him plain water before then. He gulped down a whole 180 ml!

I felt anxious about whether surgery would proceed as a few others in our bay had theirs cancelled the day before. It felt nice to have others there with us—we were all strangers but our journeys of open-heart surgery brought us together. We understood each other's pains and fears without even having to voice them.

Helen, the night nurse and I gave Saajan a bed bath with special antiseptic wash. I gazed at his bare chest and realised that was the last time I'd see it scar-free. I curbed my thoughts quickly and focused on his beautiful little face instead. His beautiful smile made it hurt that much more—he was blissfully unaware of what was about to unfold.

We settled him in his gown to prepare him for surgery. Honestly, I think that was one of the most adorable things I'd ever seen. He looked absolutely gorgeous.

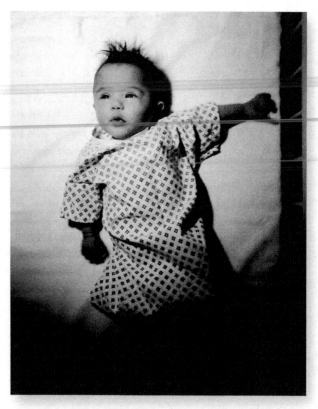

Saajan in his gown ready for open heart surgery

Preetam and Arjun arrived at the hospital by 7 am where we had cuddles and spent time as a family. Saajan was so excited to be reunited with his daddy and brother. That moment felt very still but, at the same time, there was a heaviness in my heart—would this be the last time we'd be a family? Would Saajan come out of this surgery alive? I knew all too well how quickly life can change and I feared so much that we would be robbed.

The morning of Saajan's open heart surgery

We'd explained to Arjun that Saajan would have an "ouchie" on his chest as he was having an operation. Harv had bought him a book to get him used to the idea (Usborne's "Going to the Hospital") but I'm not sure how much he really understood.

That morning felt like a daze. I was grateful that the surgery was scheduled for early in the day as it gave me less time to think. I was anxious, really anxious. It all felt surreal.

CHAPTER 20:

A Broken Heart

8.05 am. The anaesthetists came and told us to be ready in five minutes.

Nothing can prepare you for the moment that you hand your baby to a surgeon.

Suddenly, everything seemed to be moving so fast. My heart sank further as the fear of losing Saajan confronted me. Death stared me in the face. We were told that the first 24 hours post-surgery were critical and that 10 percent of babies who undergo open-heart surgery don't make it.

So many things were going through my mind.

The thought that my baby was going to be put to sleep.

The thought that he may never wake up.

The thought that something could go horribly wrong.

The thought that his precious life was in someone else's hands.

At that point, I really didn't care about him having Down's Syndrome. It was so insignificant. I just wanted him to be okay. I wanted our family to be okay. I just wanted this nightmare to be over.

As Preetam and I wheeled him down with the nurses, Saajan's eyes smiled at us through the cot bars. He looked so adorable in his little gown. Would this be the last time we'd see him smiling at us? I was so anxious to watch him be put to sleep. The anaesthetist had warned us that often, children with Down's Syndrome can be quite fussy and difficult when being put to sleep.

As we walked along the never-ending corridor, there were swarms of people in scrubs and what felt like an endless number of theatres.

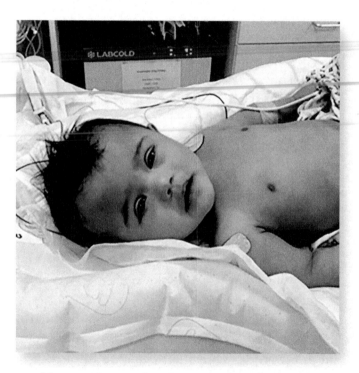

My sweet boy ready to be put to sleep for surgery

We finally reached our destination. They placed the gas mask over Saajan's mouth and Preetam and I held his hands tightly. He inhaled beautifully and didn't fight at all—breaking the stereotype that the anaesthetist had painted him with.

I felt my heart beating faster as his slowed down.

I felt my stomach in my throat and the tears came flooding out as his tight grip around our fingers began to loosen. The smile on his beautiful face faded—a picture I will never ever forget.

I cried and I cried. Not loud sobs, just silent tears streamed down my face.

He looked so beautiful, so peaceful, so perfect. I love him. I really love him.

Any doubt I had before this was erased in that moment. I cared about nothing else other than him coming out from that surgery okay. They informed us that we should receive a call in about five hours (2 pm).

I was terrified that the dark thoughts I'd had when he was born would materialise now. The guilt consumed me more than I could handle.

Preetam and I clung on to each other in our helpless states—we both knew it was only us who could understand this journey. Neither of us said anything but we understood everything. We are his parents. This is our journey. This is our reality. He is our flesh and blood. He is ours.

We headed upstairs to meet my sister Goov and Arjun. I felt some relief on seeing Arjun. Knowing we had to put on a brave face for him gave us a purpose, something else to focus on. He was our biggest strength and he didn't even know it.

We headed back to the hotel where we'd planned on taking Arjun swimming as a distraction. Sarah had advised us to go out and do something to keep our minds busy. I fell asleep so we didn't end up going swimming. I woke up feeling confused and like I'd just had a bad dream.

Nope, it wasn't a bad dream.

This was real.

My son was probably wide open at the chest right now. It was terrifying to know his heart would be on a bypass machine and that he wouldn't be breathing by himself.

We got ready and decided to head out for brunch. It was a good distraction. After brunch, we went for a walk in South Kensington. There were a lot worse locations we could be in! It had come up to five hours and we still hadn't received a phone call. I began to stress. What if something had gone wrong?

2.15 pm…

2.30 pm…

2.45 pm…

3 pm…

3.15 pm… I called the hospital; it had been well over six hours. PICU still hadn't heard anything. He was still in theatre. Why was it taking so long? I began acting out. I didn't want to talk to anyone; I felt sick. I became snappy. I needed the others to manage Arjun as he was unable to distract me anymore. I just needed to know that Saajan was okay.

3.30 pm…

3.45 pm…

4 pm… Preetam finally received a call. We ran from South Kensington back to the hospital. My legs felt like jelly and I felt like I was going to collapse. I felt like something was pushing against my chest and I couldn't breathe. I didn't have time for a panic attack. I needed to get there. Now. It was the longest seven hours of my life, especially the last two. Goov entertained Arj while we returned to the hospital. She took him for an ice cream and they went swimming—he was oblivious to what was going on.

We waited patiently in the parents' room for the surgeon to debrief us while they settled Saajan post-surgery. Mr Michielon came and took us to a private room. "Is he ok?" was my immediate question. He smiled and said, "Yes". If you ever have the pleasure of meeting Mr Michielon (for a reason other than your little one requiring open-heart surgery!!), you'll notice his cool and soothing nature. It has an immediate calming effect. He explained the surgery to us—it went a little over my head, to be honest. Preetam asked a few questions (he's the technical one).

Overall, the surgeon was happy with the surgery. It ended up being more complicated than anticipated. He described how they repaired the defect—I was in awe of their knowledge and ability to think on the spot. Saajan's heart was the size of a walnut. To perform such intricate surgery is an art. How could I ever repay this man and his team for saving my child's life?

He was pleased with Saajan's immediate condition post-surgery—he was on the lowest dose of medication. "That's our boy!" we thought. They felt he'd be able to be extubated (taking out the tube that helps you to breathe) that same evening when he woke up. We were so excited.

We were finally able to see him. I couldn't wait. I was so glad Sarah had shown me pictures of Oscar post-surgery so I knew what to expect. It may have come as quite a surprise had I not. There were lots of tubes, wires and machinery and it could be quite daunting.

We saw him through the window looking so peaceful. He looked so sweet. So pure. We were relieved to be reunited. He was still heavily sedated and sleeping peacefully.

I was relieved to meet Nektaria, his nurse for the remainder of the day. I immediately felt at ease. The nurses are incredible. They possess an abundance of knowledge and the hearts of angels. We spent a few hours with Saajan literally staring at him in awe. How is it that someone so small has endured so much? We were so happy with his progress but our hearts weighed heavily with how much he'd already had to suffer in his short life.

As the evening progressed, Saajan wasn't showing much sign of waking up. It was looking more likely that they wouldn't be able to extubate him that day but that was okay. It just meant he could rest a little longer. As gutted as I was that we wouldn't get to see his beautiful eyes tonight, I was just relieved that the surgery was over.

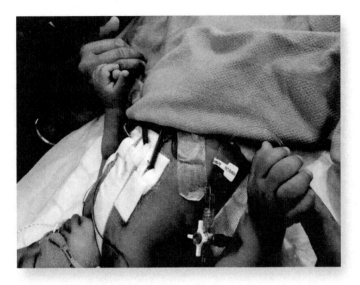

Saajan post open heart surgery

Preetam with Saajan post open heart surgery

We met the night nurse, Laura. Another beautiful soul. Laura assured us that if there was any need to, they'd call us straight away during the night. We also asked if they could call us if he showed any sign of waking up as we wanted to be there when he opened his eyes. The PICU nurses encouraged us to spend time with Arjun while Saajan was there as he had one to one care and there wasn't a lot we could do, whereas Arjun probably needed us more.

I felt comfortable leaving Saajan in the nurse's care to pop out for dinner with the others. We made sure we went out for lunch and dinner—it was a break for us and also family time to focus on Arjun.

CHAPTER 21:

The Rollercoaster that Followed

WE WENT TO SLEEP REALLY content and happy that night. I couldn't stop thanking God and thinking about the amazing people who had made this possible. Life felt good. It felt—positive. It helped having the twins stay overnight with us. The doctors had warned us that the first 24 hours are critical and that we could be called in at any time. Not having the twins around would have made it difficult to rush to the hospital had we needed to do so with Arjun. We were so grateful to have them.

I woke up the next morning and called the hospital.

"We're really sorry," we were told. "Saajan woke during the night but immediately, his heart rate and temperature shot up and we had no choice but to sedate him and give him medication to paralyse him and to bring the heart rate and temperature down."

It felt like my heart stopped beating. What had happened?! What did this mean? Was he going to survive?! I was terrified.

Guilt washed over me. He must have been so scared when he woke up without us there. Parents are not permitted to sleep overnight in PICU.

We were told that Saajan would be monitored and their main thing was to keep him stable. They were waiting for him to wake up to see how he was this time around.

We quickly got ready, had a hurried breakfast and rushed to the hospital. Literally, as we were rushing to his room, he began stirring—it was like he waited for us. He briefly opened his eyes and clenched our hands. It felt so nice to feel life in him again. My heart felt full. My beautiful boy was waking up.

By mid-morning, he was opening his eyes more frequently and moved from fully assisted breathing (BIPAP) to CPAP where he could breathe a little by himself. I was so proud of him! As I gradually saw the statistic on the screen show his level of breathing versus the machine's support, I was doing a silent happy dance. It was hard to see him cry without any noise because of the tube. I was so desperate to see his smile and hear his little voice again. I missed it so much. I prayed hard to God to forgive me for all the dark thoughts I'd had when he was born—I so badly wanted him to be okay.

I decided to get some pictures printed to place in Saajan's bed so he could see us always—one of Guru Nanak Dev Ji, one of us at the seaside and one of him and Arjun. Goov and I roamed Old Brompton Road searching for a picture printing shop—I was so used to doing this online, it felt nostalgic to do it in person! I also got Arjun one printed of Saajan to keep with him.

By the afternoon, Saajan was ready to be extubated from oxygen. I was nervous about this as I figured he'd probably struggle for a few breaths and may splutter. But it was a huge milestone.

It was a relief to hear his little cry. He was quite hoarse but the familiar sound of his tiny voice gave me so much comfort. He could cry freely. He was still really sleepy. We were so desperate to see him smile. We missed his voice—he's our daily alarm clock in the mornings and the sound of him babbling and giggling was the sweetest sound to wake up to.

As the day progressed, the nurses noticed that Saajan's heart rhythm was flipping between nodal (abnormal) and sinus (normal). This is basically where the heart's electricity supply is being generated from the centre because of the location of the AVSD (nodal) instead of the upper right side where it should be (sinus). His heart rate had also accelerated (up to 180).

I panicked. "What if he has a heart attack?"

They placed Saajan on a temporary pacemaker to regulate his rhythm. That then became the focus—to fix his arrhythmia. I was told it's a common complication post-surgery and should settle. I couldn't help but worry. We were told that if it didn't fix itself, they'd try medication and if that didn't work, the last resort would be to fit a pacemaker. I felt helpless, anxious and sad. As we took a step forward, it felt like we took two back. I realised that

I needed to take a moment at a time and pray for the best—that was the whole reason he was in PICU.

It really helped to be surrounded by three other lovely families. By the end of our stay in hospital, we'd become like one big family. You're all going through the same or similar journey and everyone "gets it". We had so many laughs and we were there to lean on each other as we rode the hurdles together. I was praying for every single child there.

As Saajan had been extubated, although he still had several tubes in, we decided to allow Arjun to come and see Saajan. I'd shown him pictures the night before and he seemed okay. Preetam and I had made the conscious decision to always be as transparent as possible with Arjun while also considering he was still at the tender age of almost three. Given hospital appointments and surgeries were very much a part of our new lives, it wasn't something we wanted to shield Arjun from entirely. We spoke about the operation and although he didn't comprehend the whole thing, he knew Saajan needed the doctors' help to be fixed. I also wanted him to understand that mummy and daddy weren't missing because they were out having fun—Saajan needed us right now.

He arrived bushy-tailed and very excited to see his little brother after spending the afternoon at Harrods with Goov. He came excitedly bearing gifts for Saajy—a bright orange dinosaur. I wasn't prepared for his reaction. He was quiet. Really quiet. Perhaps absorbing what on earth was happening—trying to understand why his brother looked so different?

Reunited as a family

As he tried to take in his unfamiliar surroundings, I quickly diverted his attention to the book that we'd been reading to him, "My Brother Is Having an Operation". He warmed as he related the situation in front of him back to the book. He started gently talking to Saajan.

Though Saajan was still in and out of sleep, he responded to the sound of Arjun's voice. I struggled to fight back my tears as I watched my two sons. I remember scanning Arjun's face the whole time he was there, a smile hiding a thousand emotions as he just didn't know how to process it. Just a few days ago, he and his brother had been playing, cuddling and kissing. How had I ever assumed that they'd have no relationship? They had become each other's heartbeat.

As we walked out into the corridor to take Arjun back to the hotel, he broke down and wailed, "I want my brother! I want my brother! I want my brother to come home!!" We stood in the corridor as I tightly embraced Arjun and Preetam embraced me and we sobbed loudly as our hearts yearned for normality to be restored. We just wanted to be reunited as a family again. Arjun cried loudly from the pit of his stomach. I felt helpless as a mother, with one son lying there at the mercy of the Almighty for his life and one so badly wanting his brother to still be how he knew him. I just wanted to fix things for both of them, but I was helpless. It was something we had to ride out as a family. My heart felt shattered for Arjun. The sound of his cries will forever haunt me.

On subsequent visits, Arjun was much calmer and enjoyed spending time with his brother and the others in our bay. He also became a pro at the correct way of washing hands (including elbows!) and would prep the family when they came to visit. Who knew that these skills would come in handy for the future global pandemic that we'd be facing!

Going through the daily highs and lows, it helped having the twins by our side—they were there to do anything we needed, be it having a Nutella crepe for comfort, babysitting Arjun, or running home to do our washing. They made a crap situation bearable with some moments of laughter.

I walked to the hospital daily from our hotel—it was about a 15-minute walk and I absolutely loved that part of my day where I got to enjoy the beauty of Kensington. Our hotel was located opposite the V&A which boasts such beautiful architecture. I loved taking in the morning hustle and bustle. I loved seeing all the cute cafés, some of which we visited when popping out for a break from the hospital. I admired the large and proud front doors—I had serious front-door envy—and just generally inhaling the beauty of London. This was something I'd never have experienced had we not been going through all of this with Saajan. I took any opportunity I had to walk during our stay because I loved what I saw at every turn. Silver linings—taking the beauty in at each and every moment we could.

It was such a great suggestion from Preetam and made such a huge difference to our stay and experience as a whole. It also meant that Arjun was occupied—we weren't going to let this situation destroy us. We wanted to make the best out of a bad situation and we definitely did. With the twins by our side, Arjun got to see so much while in London with his masis from London Zoo to the Science Museum to being spoilt with lots of ice cream!

Once we arrived back at the hospital, Saajan was agitated. I knew right away it was because he was hungry. After a few days of nil by mouth, his hunger was starting to return. I knew it was hunger more than pain—call it mother's instinct! He was being a little pickle and trying to pull his drains out. I felt for him as I can't imagine being hooked up to so many wires and tubes. I also can't imagine how painful it must be. In a way, it was good to see the little fighter back—he looked so precious. We were starting to get our little boy back.

As the day progressed, Saajan's heart rate became accelerated again so they decided to give him some medication to stabilise it. He was still shifting in and out of nodal and sinus rhythm. I clung onto hope and coped the only way I know how—I prayed.

That day, while with Saaj, I heard the emergency buzzer go off and suddenly saw everyone run. It was so scary. My heart sank as I feared what was unfolding in the room next door.

Sadly, the baby passed away. I didn't know the family but I could only imagine their pain and anguish. It suddenly became very real what a scary place PICU is. There are so many children with so many different conditions and complications—doctors work miracles, but sadly, not everyone gets to take their baby home. I longed to hold Saajan and cuddle him.

During the doctor's ward round that evening, she spotted a milky fluid in one of Saajan's drains. I didn't know what this meant at the time but as she spoke, Preetam did what they tell you not to do—he turned to Dr Google.

Chylothorax.

As I read up on it, I felt sick, devastated and terrified. It's basically when there's a little tear on the lymph duct during surgery and it begins to build up fatty fluid.

Google told me it was a high-risk complication and there's a mortality rate of 10 percent. Again, a statistic that wasn't in my favour compared to the one in 100,000 one I had for a baby with Down's syndrome.

They were going to take a sample of the fluid and send it off for confirmation. Deep down, I knew that our suspicions were right and that it definitely was chylothorax.

I felt similar to how I did when receiving Saajan's diagnosis.

Weak.

Withdrawn.

Terrified.

Anxious.

I was unable to communicate with anyone. I wasn't even able to take comfort in Arjun's embrace. I just wanted Saajan to be okay. I wanted him to be alive.

This day was the worst during our whole stay in hospital. The combination of witnessing a family lose their precious angel plus a list of complications post-surgery really took its toll on me. I didn't cope well that night.

I stayed awake all night and called the hospital a few times. I cried a lot that night—a pain that I couldn't even articulate, a fear that grew with each breath that I took.

Arjun would cry for Saajan every bedtime. He would kiss Saajan's picture good night every evening and every morning hugging it tightly. That night, I slept with Saajan's picture next to me and uncontrollably sobbed throughout the night. I felt mentally and emotionally shattered. My stress began to manifest physically—I had tummy cramps and my heart was racing. I couldn't stomach food and the walk to the hospital didn't feel as beautiful as it usually did.

By the time I reached the hospital (it felt like forever), they had the lab results—it was confirmed. He did have chylothorax. The plan was to put him on fat-free milk for four to six weeks to give the tear a chance to heal. I'd read about how children had become malnourished and I was terrified of what this meant for Saajan, however, I also knew I had no other choice.

I was informed that most children hate monogen (fat-free milk) and that he was unlikely to take it orally so may need to be tube-fed.

The speech and language therapist visited us to watch Saajan drink his milk. She felt he may have some feeding issues which was yet another hurdle to cross. I felt a little frustrated as I wasn't sure where my focus was supposed to lie—on the chylothorax or his feeding. I couldn't do both. She felt he would be better solely tube-fed. Mother's instinct dictated otherwise. Thankfully, the doctors also agreed with me—they were keen to continue Saajan on the bottle and not regress to tube-feeding for now.

He took his first and second bottle fine but by the third, he was refusing it orally so we switched to tube-feeding. It felt like we were going backwards.

As each day unfolded, it felt like we were presented with a new challenge.

The next day, Saajan's heart was still flipping between nodal and sinus rhythm but they assured me this is common and it should settle.

His drain was leaking a lot less—I was thrilled! He'd gone from draining 100 ml and 90 ml, to 50 ml and 35 ml. I prayed hard that the monogen would work. They struggled to feed him by bottle during the night, so they tube fed. I was adamant about getting him off the tube and back onto the bottle.

Saajan was so emotional when he saw Preetam. He was a lot more alert now—he craved a cuddle but we couldn't because of the drains. He was pleased to see his grandparents, and Pua too, who were relieved to see him.

The tubes visibly looked like they had a lot less fluid in them and I felt much better and more hopeful that day.

By the following day, Saajan was doing really well; he'd been in sinus rhythm for 24 hours and they'd taken him off his heart rate medication and he was coping well, though it was creeping up.

We were also able to have his drains removed that day as they were pleased with the chyle clearing up. We were able to hold our baby boy for the first time since he had surgery and it felt so good! We had lots of smiles and giggles and it felt like we had our boy back! It was an emotional time and it was such a huge comfort seeing how much comfort Saajan took from our embrace.

Preetam was also able to feed him about 30 ml orally from a bottle. Progress!

Towards the evening, the doctor was concerned that his leg looked a little swollen and they suspected he may have a blood clot. ARGH!

By this time, the other families in our bay were also further along in their journey and everyone was a little

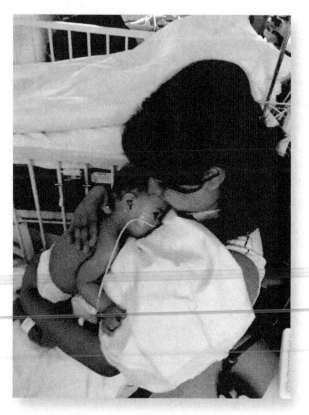

Finally able to hold Saajan and it felt so good!

more settled. We were lucky to have such a fab bunch during our stay. As some of the others were ready to leave, it felt very bitter-sweet. We'd all been in a pretty horrible situation, but we had some fond memories too. We formed a little family as we watched the resilience of our little ones, laughed, cried, and ate lots of cake!

Goov and I went for lunch in the hospital canteen one afternoon—chunky chips and beans were the ultimate comfort food. As we sat there, she said, "Harps, I think we should cancel our engagement". We both broke down. She was due to have her Indian engagement ceremony (chunni) in just two weeks. The time when she should have been busy celebrating and looking forward to her upcoming event she had spent being by Arjun and Saajan's side. "No," I said, "you're going ahead with it!" as I silently prayed that my son would still be alive then. I felt overwhelmed—my sisters had been so selfless.

Goov's priority was Saajan even when I'd tried to discuss her chunni plans, Harv couldn't bear to be far from us and stayed the entire week in London with us. I was overwhelmed by the kindness of their employers— for flexing the rules and allowing them to be by our side. Their act of kindness went beyond what they ever could have imagined.

By the sixth day in PICU, all our friends had left. It felt really sad. We were thrilled that they'd moved on in their journeys but it felt lonely and quiet. Time seemed to pass a lot slower too. We were also grateful that Saajan was stable too and that the biggest concern was now his feeding.

We were torn between the doctors and the SALT—the SALT was encouraging tube-feeding whereas the doctors were adamant on ensuring he got back on the bottle. The predicament, we believed, was the taste of the milk.

To test the theory, and because they were pleased with the reduction in his chyle output, the doctors weighed up the situation and decided to revert Saajy back onto SMA to see if it was the milk he disliked, or if it was that he no longer liked the bottle. I prayed to God it was just the taste of the milk. We'd never had feeding issues prior to this and it wasn't an additional battle we needed.

On the SMA, I managed to feed Saajan 55 ml and Preetam managed a whopping 95 ml! The doctors were right—it was the taste of the milk.

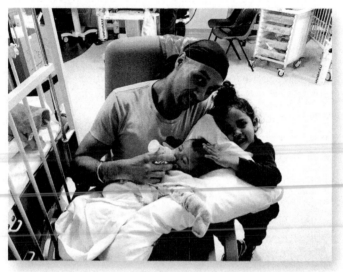

Saajan having a taste of SMA after being on monogen

Given we'd initially been told Saajan would require monogen for at least four to six weeks, I felt uneasy about switching back. The doctors felt comfortable that it was the right decision and assured us they'd monitor his lungs and chest.

After six nights in PICU, we were finally moved to the ward to our own private room (because that was the only bed available!).

Saajan was taking his bottle really well and, slowly, his feeds began to increase. He was super-hungry and feeding more frequently. They did a chest x-ray the night before and were happy with how it looked.

It was my first night staying at the hospital now that we were on the ward and I felt quite lonely. Perhaps the enormity of the situation was finally dawning on me. I found myself feeling very withdrawn and emotional. I missed Preetam and Arjun who had now returned home. I longed for us to finally be a family again.

Preetam put a smile on my face when he told me that he and Arjun had slept on the edge of our bed as he had refused to let Preetam sleep on "Mummy's side"—it melted my heart!

The doctor felt they wanted to monitor Saajan for another 24 hours but I managed to convince them to let us go and see him as an outpatient instead. I felt he was in much better spirits and going home would probably do him a lot more good than being at the hospital.

They agreed to do his discharge tests and if all looked okay, they'd let him go and see him as an outpatient.

All looked good for now!

Saajan's NG tube was removed and we were finally able to see his beautiful face again!

Home time!

I decided to surprise Preetam and Arjun with the news that it was home time when they arrived to visit us—I've never seen Preetam smile so much! We were all buzzing with excitement. We were all so relieved to finally be able to be back together as a unit.

CHAPTER 22:

Back to the Future

THE DIFFERENCE IN HOW WE felt returning home with Saajan after open-heart surgery compared with when he came home after being born was so stark that it was impossible for us to not notice. We felt relieved, we felt hopeful, we felt grateful, we felt blessed, we felt calm, and we felt elated. We felt different.

We felt proud.

Pride. It was a feeling I didn't think I'd ever associate with Saajan when he was first born.

I loved him.

The veil of fear and misjudgement was finally starting to lift and I was experiencing that same love that I felt when he was first born when I was oblivious to what was about to unfold.

Despite having been through so much since he entered this world, he fought through with a smile on his face when he could through the most painful time. He had taught us so much in such a short time. We were no longer who we

Back home

were back then. In this moment, it felt so obvious as to why he was sent to us; as a gift, as our teacher. We felt the same about Arjun—he had handled the situation so well and his innocence and love for Saajan taught us how we should be. That realisation felt like an epiphany.

When we first found out about the surgery, I felt so much anger. Why was my little boy having to go through so much? When was this going to stop? After the surgery,

Our little superstar

I had a moment of clarity; like someone had shaken the negativity and sadness out of us. Saajan is my son; the protective maternal instinct rose from the deepest part of my heart. What I didn't know at that time was that we absolutely *had* to go through that trauma to be able to move forward—it was the pivotal point in our journey of acceptance. My motto has always been "every cloud has a silver lining" and this was it.

I also recognised my personal growth through the situation as I reflected. The old Harps would have spent the entire time mourning while Saajan was in hospital, but through Arjun, we turned the situation on its head. My maternal instinct meant that I wanted to protect Arjun too. Though Saajan endured so much and we went through the heartbreak of watching him and feeling so helpless at times, we still managed to get some quality time with Arjun and with my sisters, exploring the pretty streets of South Kensington, surviving off of Hummingbirds brownies and widening our coffee world horizons by trying more than just Starbucks and Costa! We frequented a lovely local dessert parlour called "Scoop" during our time in South Kensington. We became familiar faces to the staff and Arjun was often gifted an extra scoop or two! When we drive through South Kensington today, our hearts aren't filled with dread but instead, they were filled with hope and also sweet memories because we chose to try and make a shit situation bearable.

While Saajan had been at the Royal Brompton, the speech and language team had suspected he may be silently aspirating—this is where fluid is travelling to the lungs when drinking. It would make him more susceptible to pneumonia and other complications. It's related to the low muscle tone associated with Down's syndrome. Had we not endured open-heart surgery, I'd have been devastated, but upon receiving the news, my first question was, "is there a solution?" When they responded, "yes", I said, "that's fine then". Perspective; something Saajan

*My sisters by our side during Saajan's open heart
surgery ensuring Arjun was also taken care of*

has taught us. We were so fortunate that he was alive. We
were given a starch powder to thicken his fluids which
enables the fluid to travel slower and to the correct place.
Is it a bit of a nuisance? A little, but we just got used to it!
In the grand scheme of things, I'm just grateful that there
is a solution and I hope he grows out of it as his body
strengthens, but if not, that's okay too.

I felt overwhelmed with gratitude to the staff at the Royal Brompton. They'd taken care of our son with so much love. If it wasn't for them, he wouldn't have received the care and comfort that he did and we'd not have received the support that we did.

My biggest heartache post-surgery was the fear that it's ingrained in Arjun's memory. To this day, if Saajan has even a slight cold, Arjun panics. We do our best to manage the situation and reassure Arjun that everything is going to be okay. We are so mindful of how he has had to witness so much more than the average five-year-old. Again, that's something that only our little unit can appreciate.

I wanted to move forward—I was ready. And I knew it was in my hands.

I had been resistant to people visiting us during the first six months of Saajan's life. I didn't have any words. After his surgery, I began to let in people that I felt "safe" around. Dina—my husband's friend's wife—met Saajan soon after he was out of hospital. She instantly fell in love with him and their connection was undeniable. She began coming over every single day to see Saajan. Her day would begin with her texting me to ask how Saajan was; anytime she felt low, Saajan was HER medicine. My son quickly became the centre of someone else's life. Through watching Dina patiently do physiotherapy with Saajan almost daily, rocking him to sleep and nurturing him so lovingly, I learnt to love my son. Where I felt like I'd failed, Dina was sent to play the role that I sometimes struggled to play. She made time for my son, my son who

Arjun, Dina & Saajan

had Down's syndrome. She didn't care about the label. Even after having her own child, Dina's love for Saajan hasn't faded. She also has a really close bond with Arjun. She is full of fun and zest.

Recently, it was Dina's birthday. When her husband Raj asked her what she'd like to do, she said she wanted to spend the day with Saajan, Arjun and her own baby (Arjun was at another party). I reluctantly agreed. He is

THAT important to her. I was a little anxious not knowing how he'd behave and if it would end up ruining their day. While they were gone, I was literally in disbelief—I never imagined anyone (other than maybe our siblings) would want to take Saajan out without us there.

I felt emotional, overwhelmed and grateful. Dina sent me pictures throughout the day and when she returned, she filled me in on what a perfect day it had been and how grateful she was that she had the opportunity to spend the day with Saajan. Dina still remains oblivious to what a profound impact her love has on our family, especially both the boys.

We got to celebrate Goov's chunni two weeks after Saajan's open-heart surgery. I was in disbelief for most of that night as the guests and my family partied away— weeks before, I wasn't sure if my child would even still be here let alone whether we'd be able to celebrate with my sister. I couldn't believe that we'd gotten through and we were there to be a part of the celebrations. I felt immensely grateful and overwhelmed and was so happy for Goov and my new brother-in-law!

At eight months, we began weekly group SALT with Sparkles. I felt sceptical about Mel, the therapist, doing phonics with Saajan at such a young age; he didn't respond. Was he even learning anything? It felt like a play session more than anything but I was so grateful for the positivity that Mel bought to our journey. As doubtful as I was, she'd celebrate any small achievement that Saajan made. We had two other children in our class with Saajan and I couldn't help but compare his progress to theirs.

Us all set to celebrate Goov masi
& Eamun masar's chunni

Was I really doing this? Now stooping to compare my child with Down's syndrome to other children with Down's syndrome knowing full well that they all develop differently just like typically developing children! I had to catch myself and refocus my attention on Saajan. Sparkles felt a lot nicer, brighter and happier than the NHS appointments. It didn't feel as claustrophobic, as mellow, as depressing. It became my happy place. As time went on, I began to enjoy it more and more.

Mel didn't only work on speech per se but also on pre-verbal skills such as eye contact, turn-taking and attention through pictures and games. For example, ready-steady-go games for turn-taking, Mr Potato Head for teaching body parts and a baby doll to teach basic care all while incorporating signs. They also worked on exercises to help strengthen muscle tone and coordination in the mouth area, for example, using different bubble wands to blow bubbles.

I remember visiting the Sparkles physiotherapist, Debbie, for the first time. She's a big personality and her enthusiasm is enough to lift anyone up! As we entered the room, I was feeling rather deflated knowing that Saajan was months off from crawling. "Oh, my goodness," she gasped, "his communication is just beautiful!" she cooed as he smiled at her. She explained to us that though it may seem like Saajan's physical development was slow, his non-verbal communication was brilliant. Debbie was full of love, passion, patience and wisdom—her love for what she does shone through at every single session.

For us, Sparkles gave us much more than just extra physiotherapy and SALT for Saajan; they uplifted us when we've felt deflated or when progress seemed slow— Debbie was always so quick to champion Saajan's victories and redirect our attention to what he HAD achieved. Starting Sparkles was like a breath of fresh air!

As time passed, I felt ready to try therapy again, but this time, I wanted to be in control of who I saw. I searched the internet for a private therapist. I stumbled upon Emilia. I'm not quite sure what drew me to

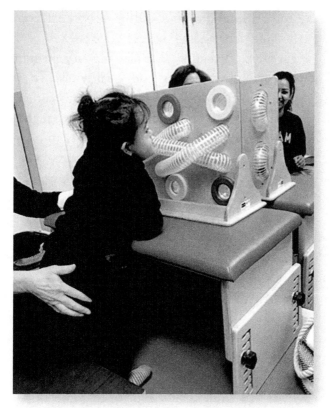

Saajan at physiotherapy with Sparkles

contacting her—maybe it was the fact that her skill set included hypnotherapy and I thought she'd be able to magic all my woes away! Shortly afterwards, I began private psychotherapy with her, and that was the start of my recovery. Although Emilia didn't have a child with additional needs, our rapport was great and I felt like she just "got me". She didn't tell me she was sorry. She didn't give me a pitiful look. She just treated me like a human

271

being and told me that it would be okay. That's what I needed—just to be treated like everyone else.

Each week, Preetam would take me on a 45-minute drive to my appointments and each week, I'd look forward to it (and not just for the delicious coffee she served me during my sessions! Haha!). She taught me how my reactions were hindering my ability to progress and we spoke about the past. She helped me to come out of my deep funk and it was a constant work in process. Knowing that I had my weekly safe space to look forward to helped me deal with the day-to-day emotions I'd face. I felt safe; I felt like I was getting somewhere. I felt lighter; life was going to be okay. Emilia was my saviour. I finally started to see the light.

As Saajan's personality evolved, the number of times we had spent mourning his diagnosis was slowly replaced by the joyful ones as we watched his fun character emerge. As he began to interact with us more and more, his diagnosis seemed less relevant. It felt like it'd taken forever for him to just smile, or for him to be more alert, but once he started coming on, we were able to get to know him for him. It helped. Strangely, much of my acceptance journey was through watching others. Watching Arjun love Saajan so unconditionally, so caringly, so dotingly, so non-judgementally taught us how we should love him. He showed us that it didn't matter that Saajan had Down's syndrome. It is just a part of him.

As much as I was growing, I still felt myself getting lost in other people's worlds. I couldn't escape them. I'd find myself feeling sad at Arjun running around with his cousins who were of the same age as Saajan, while Saajan couldn't even crawl. It stung—I so wished Saajan was running around with them too. It hurt seeing Saajan left alone to play with the grown-ups while the other kids played together. It hurt so bad. This is what I had hoped for, I had longed for—for Arjun to have a sibling to be able to do that with. It felt unfair. I feared that the brothers' relationship would be hindered by Saajan's delayed development. He loved Saajan and I had to remind myself that it was natural for Arjun to be drawn to other kids who were able to do the same things as he was. I struggled to refocus my attention on my own beautiful baby in those moments of despair.

Even after almost a year, I'd wake up some mornings and a wave of sadness would wash over me. But I knew that that moment too would pass. When I felt sad or low, I'd look straight at Saajan knowing I'd be greeted with the warmest heartfelt smile, and that always made those moments fade. He had the power to uplift my spirits— his eyes spoke for his heart. His innocence always made me feel guilty for the feelings I'd have.

Weekly therapy sessions with Emilia helped me to work through the intense thoughts I'd still have, albeit less frequently. I began feeling different, lighter, more able, more determined, stronger.

I still had my down days as I pondered over the future but they were slowly becoming outweighed by the better days.

Though I felt an abundance of support, somewhere, the feeling of judgement being passed crept up on me.

Comments or observations were taken as judgement. Preetam and I had decided from very early on that we wanted Saajan, health permitting, to have the same opportunity in life as Arjun has had. As we approached Saajan's first birthday, given his zest for life and friendly personality, we felt that he'd really enjoy nursery. My gut feeling was confirmed when Saajan attended baby crèche while Preetam and I attended sign-a-long—Saajan absolutely loved it!

"But he can't even crawl yet let alone walk!"

"How will you know if he's okay if he can't speak?" others asked.

It wasn't an easy decision as Saajan at age one was developmentally at around six months old, but we knew it was the right decision for him. Why wouldn't it be good for him to be around other peers? Why wouldn't it be good for him to get to be in a setting which promotes independence? Why wouldn't it be good for him to be in a different environment which may encourage his development further? Why wouldn't it be good for him to be around new people? There wasn't a shadow of doubt in my mind that this would be brilliant for him—this confidence of believing in myself came with time and connecting with Saajan. He's a people person and I knew he was going to love it! Had Saajan been our first child, perhaps our decision would have been different, but seeing Arjun thrive, learn and grow in a nursery setting meant we knew that it would benefit Saajan too. It also helped that we had already built a relationship with the nursery. Somewhere in the back of my mind, I did fear him being mistreated. More than him being unable to move, I was concerned about him not being able to talk to tell us.

Even before Saajan started, Arjun's nursery staff provided the family with support which has been overwhelming. In my early days, I'd often drop Arjun off, be asked how I was and end up in tears. Many of the girls were at the end of their shift but would still offer their comfort and always remind me that they were there. None of them really had to take an interest but every single one that we interacted with went above and beyond to ensure Arjun was okay and that I was ok.

It was really warming to hear how eager all the girls in the room were to meet Saajan and I knew he wouldn't disappoint!

It's so interesting that the emotions and feelings I felt with him starting were the same as when Arjun started but for different reasons. With Arjun, he was my first and it was all new to me. I was handing over my precious gift to a complete stranger that I had to trust from the start. Now that I was on to my second child, my fears with Arjun had been eradicated as I'd built relationships with his nursery so the foundation had been laid and now it was more about Saajan as a person and him getting the best out of the experience. With my typical child, I wasn't too worried about his development—I mean, I cared, but I didn't obsess. With Saajan, it felt different. I guess it's because I knew he'd find his voice a little later than Arjun did. He wouldn't be able to relay his day back to me. The level of trust and relationship-building was to another level completely—a level that terrified me.

Having a child with additional needs is definitely daunting when it comes to trusting others. Everything that needs to be considered can be overwhelming, but, more than anything, ensuring the right people are chosen to take care of your precious child is the scariest part for me. It's a bit like a lottery—luck of the draw.

They allowed Saajan to pick his own key worker by observing who he gelled with most during his settling-in sessions. This was difficult as Saajan is definitely affectionate and warms to blooming anyone!

He couldn't talk but I trusted my baby to guide me in the right direction. As much as all the girls in the room were lovely, I needed someone who had an extra love for their job and perhaps an interest in children with additional needs so that it was a mutually beneficial relationship. The fear of trusting someone with my child who had no voice yet and no mobility was paralysing at times.

Ashleigh.

Her friendly and warm persona instantly told me it would be okay. I could feel her love and interest in my son, and that, for me, was enough to know it would be the start of a beautiful relationship.

The nursery arranged a "round the table meeting" with all the key professionals in Saajan's life (his NHS speech and language therapist and physio, the nursery SENCO, his keyworker Ashleigh and the nursery manager). I walked into the meeting feeling a little apprehensive—I never imagined I'd be doing this in my life. How had our lives become so tedious? I never had to do any of this with Arjun.

As always, Arjun took my hand and held it tight (metaphorically). He woke up that morning and I asked him if he'd like to go to nursery, to which he replied "No!". When I told him it was Saajan's first day, he bounced up, rushed to brush his teeth and got ready. He lay in Saajan's cot next to him gently telling him he was starting at the same nursery as him and that he was really excited. He insisted on wearing the same hoody as Saajan too. Whatever has been thrown our way in life, God has never ever let me down in ensuring we have the right people around us to support us—Arjun's love, care and patience always save me at my weakest points despite him being a little rascal at the best of times.

On the car journey, Arjun lovingly held Saajan's hand and excitedly told him all about nursery—I found it a tad amusing given he'd usually scream the house down not to go himself. Once we arrived at nursery, Arjun eagerly darted towards the baby room with us following behind him. Saajan happily went to the nursery staff who were just as happy to receive him and Arjun, bushy-tailed, put Saajan's bag away on his coat peg—his caring and nurturing personality melted me. We asked Arjun if he'd like to stay with Saajan in the baby room but he said it was too noisy and he would prefer to go to preschool—he was satisfied that Saajan was okay.

Our meeting lasted just over three hours (Saajan's settling-in period was only meant to last an hour but he did so well!). We went through everything and I felt so much better—like a weight had been lifted off me. We discussed his medical history, his aspiration concerns, his feeding, our hopes and wishes for Saajan, his occupational therapy plan, physiotherapy plan and his speech and language plan.

With the added complexities of Saajan's aspiration, I felt so nervous and conscious that I'd be overwhelming the staff but their constant reassurance and support were incredible.

I felt excited for Saajan to embark on this new journey—I was becoming the special needs mum that I thought I'd never be! I was also grateful that we'd receive a little relief by having some of the therapy sessions at nursery instead so we'd have fewer appointments while also equipping Saajan's support network with the relevant skills to help us.

Arjun was bursting with pride that his baby brother was also at nursery. He drew him a picture which he'd folded up and put in his pocket to give to him when we got home. He also didn't want Saajan to sleep when we got home so that they could "talk" about Saajan's first day. Some of the guilt I was feeling around how Arjun was coping suddenly disappeared—he was happy. He had his greatest comfort with him at nursery now—Saajan. The nursery staff ensured the boys saw each other throughout the day.

Watching Saajan settle in at nursery so beautifully was amazing and really made me focus on the silver linings and how fortunate we were. Arjun took years to settle in; Saajan settled in right away. His carefree, go-with-the-flow attitude meant he enjoyed it for what it was. He embraced it; he went in happily every day.

While he couldn't talk, he could communicate through his mood, so I knew he was happy.

Ashleigh had patience, perseverance and so much enthusiasm with Saajan. She worked so hard to help him develop and was always so excited and vocal when he achieved a new milestone—however tiny it may have been. She'd always been proactive in understanding Saajan's additional needs—e.g., the right consistency for his fluids, or understanding his sensory needs and having the patience to try and work through them. She'd provide us with so much feedback which gave me so much reassurance knowing that Saajan was okay.

It's not often you find people with such a passion and true love—we were so grateful to Ashleigh for holding our hand and for making it easier when handing over Saajan's care to someone outside the family for the first time.

Perhaps sending Saajan to nursery and seeing that our lives were relatively "normal" calmed my nerves. It gave me the mental space to continue my life as I had always imagined. Slowly, the fact that he had Down's syndrome became less important. I felt less sorry and sad for myself.

We re-planned our trip to Punta Cana to celebrate Saajan's one-year healthy heart. We'd been on a few holidays by now, post-surgery, but this one was my favourite. The staff made it extra special and watching him play in the sand made me realise how much I'd underestimated him. The staff in the kid's club adored Saajan and would ask for him to come daily. People loved him—even strangers.

We enjoyed endless days sipping on fresh coconut water by the pool, consuming vibrant-coloured tropical fruit while lazing around and drinking in the beauty of our little family.

The staff made Saajan's healthy heart anniversary so special by providing us with a cake, filling the room with balloons and even filling the huge bathtub with bubbles and balloons for the boys.

The day we got back from Punta Cana, I was upstairs unpacking.

"HARPS!! COME DOWN!!" yelled Preetam.

"MUMMY, QUICK!!! SAAJAN'S CRAWLING!" echoed an incredibly excited Arjun!

I rushed down almost tripping over myself! I witnessed our adorable little boy crawling for the first time. 18 months it had taken but he'd done it! We were in tears; we couldn't believe the day was finally here. Finally! Sheer joy washed over us watching him achieve something so huge, knowing how difficult it was for him, and how many hurdles he had to cross, he made us feel so proud. Saajan was continuing to show us his determination.

A few months later, I returned to work. I was apprehensive about what people would be saying about me, about my child. Work felt alien as I'd been away for so long and so much had happened but I settled back in quickly enough.

Once I was out of my deep funk (courtesy of Emilia's hand-holding and a bit of mental breathing space), I felt ready to really grab my life with both hands and try to find myself again. I wasn't 100 percent okay but I was ready to just be me again.

A gentleman called Andrew contacted me just at the right time through the blog—he was trained in offering coaching sessions for a programme called *Thrive* by Rob Kelly. I was a little apprehensive at first but after having quite a lengthy telephone conversation with him, I knew it was worth a shot. The opportunity came about at the right time in my life.

Thrive is a psycho-educational program. It's like a personal trainer for your brain. 10 solid hours over 10 weeks dedicated to understanding yourself better and looking at who you are today, not the last 33 years. It focused on my foundations—my sense of power and control, my social anxiety and my self-esteem.

It required dedication through homework and committing to changing your behaviour. I was astonished by how much I changed quite quickly. People began to notice the change in me after the first two sessions.

Although we touched upon my past in *Thrive*, that wasn't the focus—I learnt that the way I look at my past on any given day depends on the lens I'm viewing it through on that day. For example, if I'm in a happy mood and I recall my wedding day, I'd think of the beautiful beach backdrop with the rainbow colours dancing at sunset. However, if I was in a bad mood, I'd recall that Preetam decided to go in a jet ski the day before our wedding and I was so upset that he'd risk his life (catastrophic much?!).

I also learnt that what we go through doesn't define us; how we choose to process it does. For example, two soldiers go to Afghanistan—Bill loses one limb and John loses three limbs. Bill comes back and wallows in self-pity for the rest of his life. However, John decides to train to be a Paralympian and becomes a gold medallist. It isn't about what you go through, it's about how you process it. Such a simple example that I remind myself of daily—I HAVE A CHOICE.

Andrew challenged my behaviour, my thoughts and my beliefs and left me equipped with the resources to challenge my own behaviour when I needed to.

Each week, I'd be given homework. I was so eager to learn that I'd look forward to the boys' bedtime so I could dedicate my time to reading this wealth of knowledge that was hitting home. It became addictive. I was committed to it because it made me feel different.

I learnt how my language was affecting my day-to-day life, and how that "negative-thinking" umbrella I'd labelled myself with could be separated further to really establish what unhelpful thinking styles I had—catastrophising and paranoia to name a few!

Having completed the course, I felt like a completely new person. Don't get me wrong, I was far from "fixed" or "perfect" but I felt like I had a new lease of life. I still had many areas of development but I felt more aware and better equipped to deal with them. It felt remarkable to see the change in me as I'd stare at my reflection in the mirror—a vast difference to those dark early days when Saajan was born. I saw how my mindset shifted and good things began happening. Or perhaps they were already happening and I was too busy viewing my life through shit-tinted spectacles?

It was the most mentally enriching thing I've ever done. It was liberating. It gave me freedom. It gave me power and it let me regain control. It elevated me.

A few months after returning to work, we were told that there would be redundancies. I was offered a secondment, but I decided to push myself out of my comfort zone and try for something new. How would I find another part-time role? I had no choice now, I had to take Saajan to SALT each Friday. I was called the same day my CV was sent to a recruiter by my friend Kat. "I have a job for you!" Paul excitedly said. "Is it part-time?" I responded. "Yes!" I was very open and honest about my situation and that I wouldn't be able to do the contracted 28 hours advertised, but I could do 20 instead. I managed to get the job—20 hours, closer to home, higher salary. The pre-*Thrive* Harps would have put that down to luck; the post-*Thrive* Harps knew that I'd put in the effort and because of that, I deserved the job.

I began going out without feeling guilty about all the things left to do at home—a guilt that most mums feel wearing the hats of many roles. I realised I've got to be okay myself to be okay for everyone else—you can't pour out of an empty cup. I focused on losing weight and eating better—the thought of Saajan being a "runner" like many kids with Down's syndrome came with its silver lining; it meant I wanted to be fitter! Having piled on four stones since pre-pregnancies, I wanted to feel good about myself again. I made a conscious effort to work on making healthier choices and the weight began to melt off. It wasn't just about losing weight; it was about feeling fitter and stronger and about taking charge.

I began going out with my friends again. I started to recognise my reflection—the familiar sight of my big hair and lips painted in my favourite lipstick, Faux by Mac. I began taking Saajan to the Gurdwara by myself—if I wanted Saajan to be a part of the community, we were responsible for integrating him. It felt daunting but the more I faced my fears, the more comfortable it became. And truth be told, he was still little. I had assumed the world would be able to see through me and my fears but I was still protected by his baby days—while he was young, no one was really going to notice the difference and by the time he grows up, I'd have grown with him.

I learnt to switch off from the world sometimes and just enjoy my beautiful family. I had the opportunity of having a six-week break between leaving my job and starting a new one—it was incredible. I went on brunch dates with myself, on day trips to London, attended a business course, walked to school with Arj, and went to India with my parents to visit The Golden Temple to feed my soul—my ultimate accomplishment. I felt so fortunate to have this time.

As I continued to share my journey on the blog, slowly but surely, our loyal following grew as many fell in love with Saajan. I was asked to host an in-person event—something that I didn't feel comfortable with at all. I didn't feel worthy! I was encouraged by my friend Kiran (who happens to be an event planner) to step outside of my comfort zone and host my first ever Baby Brain Tea 'n' Talk event where over 70 women attended and where, for the first time, I shared my story of the day Saajan was born. I couldn't quite believe the number of women who purchased tickets to come and hear our story. They were there because they cared, because they'd been on this journey with us. Standing in the room full of love, I felt like a warm blanket was being placed around me—I was terrified of sharing my rawest emotions but felt safe at the same time. It was the first time I had recounted the events that unfolded the day Saajan was born—as the tears flooded, so did my pent-up emotion. I had no idea how pivotal that talk would be in my healing journey. I had to ride the storm of all those emotions to get to a place of peace. I had to hear myself repeat my reality. For almost two years, I hadn't shared the entire story. I knew it would be emotional, but I had no idea just how emotional it would be—how the women in the room would be crying hearing my journey with me. Getting it out was liberating—as each word was spoken and left my mouth, it felt like a brick was being lifted off my shoulders.

I was writing a part of the speech while we were away on our half-term trip to Rhodes. I sat for hours in a swanky restaurant with a sea view while sipping on a hot cup of coffee as there was a gorgeous storm passing by. I felt relaxed by the sound of the rain hitting the sea. I took the opportunity to write as I felt it was symbolic of how my life felt when Saajan arrived. Towards the end of my writing, as the storm calmed, a beautiful rainbow

The Baby Brain Tea 'n' Talk Event 2018

appeared as the sun made an appearance. Again, it felt very symbolic—it felt like a reflection of my own life.

When we first received Saajan's diagnosis, I would have laughed if you'd told me I'd be hosting events and writing this book sharing my rawest, darkest, deepest emotions with the world. I didn't realise back then that our story would one day become someone else's survival guide. And here we are now!

CHAPTER 23:

Reflections & Learnings

HAVING TO FACE THE ANTAGONISING and traumatic situation of Saajan having to endure open-heart surgery was unimaginable. I still can't believe that that was part of our story—from my dreams as a little girl, to how things were unfolding, I never could have imagined.

Saajan recovering from open-heart surgery when death stared us in the face changed us, softened us. It made us realise the value of life. I was terrified that something would happen to him and that we'd lose him; that those awful thoughts I'd had when he was born would materialise. Those feelings became even more prominent when we were told Saajan had chylothorax. I understand that for many, such situations would make you question God and our faith—but for me, it was those times that strengthened my faith in God. Perhaps believing in a greater power has always been my comfort and will continue to be.

My anguish was replaced with gratitude as I came to the realisation that though life has thrown its fair share of shit at us, we've always been fortunate and blessed to have the right people around us to walk the journey with us— something that I don't take for granted but something that I had to pause and recognise. Even as our family has grown with our siblings getting married, it is comforting to see Saajan accepted and embraced with love the same way Arjun is.

Though relationships were tested, I've learnt that there will always be trials and tribulations and bumps in relationships, but ultimately, family is what has carried us through. Family doesn't have to be blood; it can be the friends that we choose.

There are also those who are sometimes unsure of how to interact with Saajan—as much as I try and hold my head up high and encourage the interaction, sometimes I can't help but feel disheartened. I often run away with those experiences and fear the future. I encourage people to ask questions if they are unsure—as uncomfortable as they may feel, it's our duty to open up conversations and educate because if we don't, who will?

For me, it's important to share education and awareness from a place of love rather than defence. I struggled with the flippant use of the word "retard"—a medical term used to describe children like mine back in the 80s. These days, the word is more commonly used as a slur. It hurts me deeply knowing that friends and colleagues have chosen to use that word as a slur, despite it being a medical term to describe Saajan. However, I have to remind myself that most people use the word flippantly and without intentional malice. Remembering this, I highlight its inappropriate use and try and use it as a chance to educate. I struggle with repeat offenders and choose to slip away from such relationships!

Why had I felt so heavy, heartbroken and full of such deep anguish with the news that my son had Down's syndrome? Was it the way in which the news had been delivered to us? With sorry looks and sombre tones filled with pitiful words? "I'm so sorry" was the initial reaction of the paediatrician—the way in which the news had been delivered very much set the tone of how we allowed ourselves to feel in those initial days, weeks and months. The power of words.

Once I came to a place of acceptance, I struggled to strike up a balance of being an advocating mum versus just being a mum. It was Nisha who reminded me that I don't have to be constantly educating and that it's okay to pick my battles. It doesn't make me any less of a mum to Saajan.

As I share more of my journey on my blog, I have more people reaching out to me to share how much they've learnt about Down's syndrome and how much Saajan and our family have changed their perception of Down's syndrome. It has been life-changing hearing from parents who feel more comfortable with a Down's syndrome diagnosis because of Saajan. I take comfort in other mothers who share their vulnerability with me—stories of cerebral palsy, life-limiting conditions and even cancer—it's made me realise how fragile life is and that I'm not alone on an unexpected journey and neither are you.

I learnt that I am often paralysed by the fear of something "bad" happening and the anxiety I create by having this fear often leads me into a state of frenzied panic. I'm more mindful of it now but I also remind myself that we've managed to deal with all the (what we thought were) "bad" things that have happened to us. When you're feeling stuck in a funk or having a bad day, remember to pause and look at how far you've come and all that you've endured through your life and the fact that you're still standing. Remind yourself that "this too shall pass".

Saajan has taught us to appreciate life and to live in the moment. One of my favourite memories is from Saajan's second birthday party. We hosted a party with a company called Mini Maniacs and Rav (the owner) ensured me that the party was specifically tailored to Saajan's interests—he loves dancing and music. We went for a space theme as the world is literally his oyster. They did such a magical job with the set-up and watching Saajan enjoy his party so much for what it was and witnessing him being so immersed in the moment was beautiful to watch. He partied like no one was watching and it made me so emotional. I received so many messages afterwards from people telling us how moved they felt watching him so content and happy; he enjoyed every single second. It's something that'll stay with me forever because it was a big lesson for us—to be present, to enjoy the NOW.

I wish I could go back and relive the first year of Saajan's life as it is such a blur now. Despite Nisha's advice to do this, in those moments, I couldn't. His first six months to a year flashed by as I wallowed in self-pity. I wish I had been more present and trusted that all would be okay and that all I needed to do was be his mum and to love him. Don't get consumed by the thought of all the appointments and therapies. They just become a part of your norm and actually, I learnt to see them as chances to spend one-to-one time with him. It's easy to become consumed by therapies and extra bits you can do for your child but remember, most importantly, our children need our love over everything. I wish I'd not spent so much time pondering over the future and instead trusted that I would just grow with it.

My experiences taught me to be kind to myself and to ride my emotions—anger, despair, denial—they're all a part of our acceptance journey. Be selfish—take time for yourself to process whatever it is you may need time to process. Channel your energy into something positive when you feel up to it—I began channelling my energy into raising awareness, by sewing, by cooking. But allow yourself to pass through every part of the process. You can't get from A to C without passing through B. There is no quick fix and the kinder you are to yourself and the less resistant you are to feeling the uncomfortable emotions, the quicker they will flow through you.

Saajan has taught me to not be so fixated on planning ahead as, despite our grand plans for life, they don't always go that way. I was someone who needed to have everything organised and planned months in advance; my Christmas shopping would be done in August! I've learnt to simplify things—to enjoy the moment for what it is without all the bells and whistles. His zero f*cks attitude is something I aspire to have! His non-judgement always, his forgiving nature and his ability to be content are aspirations for me. Saajan has taught me resilience—where I resist change, he embraces it. My advice would be to try and go with the flow! Easier said than done, I know, but if I can do it then so can you! Sometimes we've got to let life unfold and trust that it will be okay.

I also became more aware of people's energetic vibrations and their use of language and I became unapologetic for gently allowing those friendships and relationships to pass. My advice would be to trust the natural course of relationships and to see adversity and also happiness in life as a chance to evaluate your relationships. Hone in on your intuition and trust it! Energy never lies. Where we may have lost some friendships, we gained a whole lot more and the Down's syndrome community is the warmest community I've ever been a part of. Whatever your unexpected life event may be, you are not alone! Find "your people"—the cyber world has opened up our worlds even further. Saajan has helped us to sift out the valuable and unconditional friendships vs relationships that were perhaps uncomfortable with riding this journey with us. It has helped us to have a much more solid circle—fewer people but stronger relationships.

I learnt to be mindful and selective with my circle— I'm fortunate enough in that my closest friends don't feed into my negative thoughts; instead, they challenge my adverse beliefs. Sadly, human nature is such that sometimes we fuel each other's negativity without even realising it. A friend once messaged me saying she was feeling really down and quite depressed. I suggested meeting up with her local girlfriends for a little lift. She said she went for coffee with some of the other mums and felt worse. I asked her why. For me, seeing friends is often the greatest medicine as we laugh so much and I always feel lighter for it. She said there wasn't much laughing as the other ladies were also in a similar low space—the law of vibration that Vex King speaks of in his *Good Vibes, Good Life* book. They ended up sipping coffees for hours, all talking about how sad they felt. By utilising the insight that I had gained, I asked her how that was beneficial. She was surprised and said she hadn't even thought about that—that actually they were making the conscious choice to sit there and speak about all the bad stuff which, in turn, would make them feel worse. No one challenged each other's behaviour and offered a different stance. This is something I'm so grateful to Sav and Amrit—always offering me a different perspective, especially when I'm viewing life through my shit-tinted spectacles. Take a step back and review your relationships and really consider how you feel after interacting or being in the presence of your friends and family. Also, think about how others may feel being in your presence. Be wise about who you choose to surround yourself with—it is in OUR control.

I still struggle to look back at Saajan's newborn pictures without crying—those images bring back all my emotions from the time. The sight of fireworks from our windows at New Year is always a painful reminder of that day I sat in hospital, broken, while the world celebrated. I've learnt that things don't always go to plan and that we can't always control life events but we have a choice over how we react to them.

The realisation of the power of my words has been awakening. By limiting any negative feeling to this moment, not forever by using active language (e.g., "I'm making myself feel sad today by over-thinking this situation"), and by reminding myself that external events will happen but they don't determine my mood, I determine my mood based on my reaction to it, I have a choice and so do you! We get to choose the life we curate simply based on our reaction.

Instead of thinking "why is this happening to me?", I now ask myself "what is this teaching me?". It feels more empowering as it's focusing on me rather than the "life is happening to me" narrative.

I learnt that it's okay to talk about your problems and feel sad, but I remind myself that the more an experience, belief or feeling is repeated, the stronger it becomes—this is true of both negative and positive beliefs. The more we repeat negative beliefs, the more we scan for things that support those beliefs. It becomes a confirmation bias. For example, Saajan's development—if I had continued to focus on the fact that he couldn't walk, I'd be making myself feel low and would constantly scan for all the other kids that are walking at his age. Instead, I remind myself that although he can't walk, he can get about by bum-shuffling and crawling. We get to choose how we view a situation.

I've learnt to focus on the silver linings. Saajan may not be able to speak full sentences but he can most certainly communicate with us through a combination of sign language, pointing, body language and the little speech that he does have! For us, he's progressing and that's the main thing—we don't look at what pace and speed he achieves something, we just look for growth and celebrate that! He's growing and we are happy with that. His free spirit and determination leave us in awe!

I've learnt to trust the process. As much as I feared what their relationship would be when we received Saajan's diagnosis, my heart swells with the exact amount of love when I watch Arjun and Saajan together. Their bond is forever full, although, as Saajan is advancing, so are the typical sibling squabbles! Arjun is Saajan's greatest cheerleader. He wakes up every morning saying behind gritted teeth, "Mummy, he's so cute! I love him so much! I'm so lucky to have him as my brother." My prayers are that he continues to feel this way about Saajan. They are each other's comfort, each other's instant calm and each other's protectors. We can't tell either of them off without the other getting involved to defend their brother— even if the source of the argument is them! They play Hot Wheels and Avengers together and they love a good wrestle with their daddy—all the things I'd imagined as I'd caressed my blooming belly whilst pregnant with Saajan. It's wonderful to watch Saajan mimic and learn from Arjun (wish we could select the parts he absorbs though, haha!). He loves motorbikes just like Preetam and loves pizza like me! He is more like us than different! If you're reading this book because you have just received an unexpected diagnosis, ride the motions, but trust that it will all be ok! I know right now it may not feel like it, and I know my words will feel empty, but I promise you, it will be okay.

Saajan & daddy on daddy's motorbike

I've learnt not to allow my reactions to be entirely emotion-led. Arjun does have his moments of questioning Saajan's diagnosis especially as he's getting older and he's becoming more aware. He was recently uptight one morning; I asked him what was wrong and he replied, "I hate the nurse for giving my brother Down's syndrome. I want him to run around after me." We explained to Arjun that Saajan is just like everyone else except he takes a little bit longer to learn things and that he needs his brother and friends to support him. Does it hurt when he says these things? Of course. Am I grateful he says them? Yes. Because we want him to feel comfortable enough to be open and honest with his emotions and feelings and to be able to help him work through them. It's a delicate subject and one that will take him a while to understand. It's important to detach yourself from the situation and be compassionate—towards yourself as well as others! Love and frustration can co-exist.

Arjun has also become a pro and learns alongside Saajan so they are able to communicate with each other. Anytime Saajan learns a new sign, Arjun is ecstatic! His exposure to the world of additional needs has made him a soft and an emotionally intelligent little boy from a young age.

A boy in Arjun's class who happens to have autism really took a shine to Arjun and vice versa. Sometimes, this sweet boy can feel a little frustrated as he's not always able to communicate what he wants or how he feels. Arjun told me that this little boy sometimes struggles at school and he thinks he has a "little bit of Down's syndrome".

His innocence amazes me and his compassion warms my heart.

We invited this little boy over to our house for a play date—I knew how much it would mean to his mum being a mum of a child with additional needs. Arjun set up the play date so differently to how he does with his other friends. He let his friend lead and asked him what he'd like to play, whereas with his typically developing friends, he may express what he'd like to do first. I was in awe of watching him with this friend! I pray his natural instinct to be inclusive and compassionate always remains.

Arjun and Saajan do their version of kirtan together—regular things that I'd always hoped my two kids would do together while blissfully unaware of the reality while I was pregnant with Saajan. Despite thinking my reality was shattered, they are doing the things I'd hoped and longed for.

Saajan absolutely loves kirtan and without a doubt, he has some sort of soulful connection to God. It's been apparent since he was little. We recently started Arjun at tabla classes and his teacher, Sunny, messaged me saying he loved our Instagram page. I flippantly replied, "Saajan loves tabla; it's a shame the odds are against him". He replied, "Kids like Saajan are often gifted, Harps. I work with a lot of kids in schools. They think differently when it comes to music. I'm a music therapist"… He then went on to say, "Let me show you what your beautiful little boy can do, Harps. He will be playing in kirtan for sure". I couldn't believe what I was reading!

Someone wanted to teach my child tabla! Someone had faith in him! Something that I never ever imagined possible; someone wanted to try. We are going to wait until Saajan is a little older before we start. It literally feels like a dream come true and it proves that the world really is his oyster. It may just take a little longer for us to search for the correct channels but in some cases, they'll just fall in our lap! Be open to receiving and don't write your entire life off because of an unexpected event.

I realised that no matter how rubbish I may wake up feeling some days, waking up, showering and getting dressed is imperative—even when it feels like the equivalent of climbing a mountain (I'm not big on exercise!). Wake up each morning and do something that makes you feel good even when you don't feel like it.

I learnt that sleep is so important to mental health and to accept help when I need it. I learnt this lesson when I became a first-time mother with Arjun even where it meant we made the difficult decision to give up breastfeeding. As uncomfortable as it may feel, allow those around you to make things a little less hard and always pick what is right for YOU and your family.

The importance of reaching out and speaking to a professional isn't a sign of weakness—it's a sign of strength. It's okay to sometimes need a third person to help you figure shit out. Find something that works for you—for me, it was psychotherapy and *Thrive*. Along with the professionals, I enjoyed going for brunch with a best friend, a cinema date with the family on the weekend or having a family film night at home. What works for me may not work for you—find what does work for you and roll with it!

I've learnt that my past doesn't define me—it's how I choose to view it and how I choose to live my life today that does. I only need to recall *Thrive*'s analogy of the soldiers to remind myself of this. Don't get me wrong, I still have awful days and that's okay too! But I reframe my thoughts and don't allow them to reside for longer than necessary. A good friend, Pardeep, once shared a great way to approach heavy feelings—welcome them in like guests, entertain them for a short while and politely allow them to leave! It's something I remember any time I feel low.

I learnt the importance of processing the positives—it's so easy to view the world through shit-tinted spectacles when you're having a rubbish day. Write down the things that make you feel good from the last two weeks and keep reading the list and adding to it. For me, it's simple things like someone giving way to me on the road (I'm a simple gal!), to going for a family walk in the fields.

As time has passed, I focus more on today than looking too far into the future. This wasn't something that came naturally to me; it was something I had to learn for my own sanity. I knew if I was to survive this journey, I needed to find a sound balance. The stark reality of Saajan's heart surgery helped with that. I knew that not everything was in my control and I had to accept it. Clearly, life has its own plan no matter how much I try to steer it! Saajan has taught me to stop in my tracks when running away with my thoughts and to bring myself back to reality.

Both boys have taught me depth and the danger of being superficial. I was so obsessed with Saajan's Down's syndrome features that I let it rob me of precious moments with him. My tiger stripes on my belly are a reminder that my body housed my two beautiful boys and they both love cuddling up to it. I learnt to love my Harry Potter-esque scar on my forehead from the car accident—it's a reminder of what I've been through and what I've overcome.

I feel like there is so much we've learnt from both of our boys—different lessons but equal in weight. One has taught us to love unconditionally and to see through difference and one has taught us to live in the moment and just be content.

I've realised that actions speak louder than words, but intention speaks louder than action. Do people do things for the right reason? Or if someone does something that feels like they've let you down, have they meant to? Those people who said they were "sorry" when Saajan was born, was it their intention to hurt me? Probably not. Always consider the intention behind the action.

As Saajan is growing, and the gap is widening, we are facing rising challenges such as ensuring his educational needs are met. We are doing the soul-destroying task of the Education, Health and Care Plan (EHCP) to obtain funding for Saajan to have the relevant support required in an educational setting for him to be able to access the curriculum. As much as Saajan is happy to go to nursery, we know ourselves that he needs the support to be able to learn and grow. It is about fairness and Saajan being able to access the curriculum in the same way his typically developing peers may be able to. Saajan requires one-to-one support to help him understand what is required of him. The EHCP is a gruelling process and we were fortunate in that Sparkles helped fund an external company, Emma Hopkins Consultancy, to assist in completing the process. My advice would be—where you can, seek the support of professionals if possible. You don't have to face every battle alone.

Saajan tries so hard but it may just take him a little longer—from copying Preetam using a screwdriver, to mimicking me doing bath time on his own baby doll, to copying how Arjun plays with his figurines. He is so eager to learn and I have never met such a determined little boy. Even when he's tired, he will grab both of your hands and ask you to walk him around the room for as long as he can. His growth in speech amazes me—he's able to speak about 50 words and it's forever growing. Hearing his sweet voice speak words is so encouraging. We look at growth, not time. At two and a half, he's still not yet walking but he will get there! As tempting as it is to compare your child, focus on *their* journey.

It's important for me to share with you my learnings and the advice I have based on my experience because when I was amidst the chaos and where I felt like "life was happening to me", I couldn't see it. I want you to know that whatever it is that you may be going through, it will be manageable AND doable… it's going to be okay! You will look back at that to-do list at that one task filled with emotion and "burden" which now has a big fat tick next to it and know that YOU did that.

Chapter 24:

Enlightened

When I look back on where we were just a few years ago, compared to where we are now, I'm in awe. I feel like a phoenix that has risen. My outlook is so different to what I could ever have imagined when I first became a mother, and later, when we had Saajan.

"Just when the caterpillar thought the world was over, she became a butterfly" (Chuang Tzu) captures it perfectly. I may have a few scuffs on my wings but I'm flying. I can see past the label that has been placed on Saajan. I see a future.

Saajan's future still worries me and those initial questions I had when he was born still creep up on me but these thoughts are far less than they were when he was first born. As time has gone on, and I've met more adults with Down's syndrome, my worries have eased.

In the summer of 2018, I was contacted by a lady via my Facebook page. She told me she manages accommodation for those with additional needs and there was someone she'd like me to meet—Will. Will swims for Great Britain with Down's Syndrome Swimming GB. They have European and World Championships every year for which Will has won a number of medals. I was really nervous but I knew it was something I absolutely had to do. I remember pulling up outside and feeling nervous. "How would I speak to Will? Will he know what I'm saying?" I then remembered that Will was no different to Saajan and that I'd want people to treat him just like they would anyone else and that's exactly what I did. Will showed me his room, we hung out and spoke about his swimming, our favourite food and his friends.

Will religiously wakes up at 5 am three times a week to train for swimming competitions where I can't even swim and the only reason that I'd ever wake up at 5 am is because of my children!! He's travelled to so many destinations I hope to visit! He loves science, has a big friendship circle and loves Chinese food.

Will lives in shared accommodation with the most amazing support workers who are basically there just in case Will needs a little help (or a little push) with anything. Otherwise, he lives a very independent, fulfilling and successful life as highlighted above. He travels alone (both on a plane and frequently the bus), he goes away on holiday without his family and, oh my goodness, his bedroom is spotless! I hope my boys are like that at 24! To be honest, Down's syndrome came into it very little other than my admiration for how he has thrashed all the stereotypes associated with having Down's syndrome—fears I had when Saajan was born.

Down's syndrome hasn't held him back one single bit. Behind Will is his loving and supporting family. They've always encouraged and supported him in whatever he's wanted to do. As Ali (Will's mother) said, "We put no ceiling on Will's life,"—something I'll remember forever. Saajan will achieve whatever his heart desires; we will never let a label hold him back.

The support workers I met were the most wonderful souls. You could see completely their love for their job. In fact, it didn't feel like they were there to do "a job", it felt like they were there as friends. As Iza said, "We aren't here to live their lives for them, we're just here to support them if they need it". I found Will's presence and his zest for life, his commitment to swimming and his achievements in life so inspiring. Some people have such a lovely aura and good energy—Will's one of those. I'm so grateful I had the privilege of meeting Will. That meeting changed so much for me—it restored my faith for the future. We live in a world where so much support and opportunity exist compared to the sixties and seventies. This isn't a journey you have to walk alone.

Before I was consumed by worries like, "will he ever be independent?" but now my biggest worry is how he'll be treated by other humans. Meeting people like Amber restored my faith in humanity and reassured me that good people do exist. Meeting Will has shown me that Saajan has every chance of living independently and I have no doubt that he will want to one day.

Saajan has been involved in various campaigns where people near and far have shared campaign posters from hospitals to big banks to libraries. He has been on the news and been spotted in and around town from his posters—he has made a greater difference in his short life than some do in their entirety!

I have had friends, family members and even strangers tell us how they feel Saajan has helped heal them or that his presence provides them with an instant calm and warm feeling. Dina is the greatest example of this.

Dina & Saajan

Wherever we go, there is someone who will be drawn to him in a really special way—a way that even they can't describe. Perhaps it's his infectious smile and the twinkle in his eye! To think that I grieved so hard when he was born is crazy. Now, I feel so grateful to be the mother of this divine little human! I have no doubt that he will continue to touch those he encounters.

He is so much more than a little boy with Down's syndrome—that is just a small part of him. Would I change the fact that he has Down's syndrome? Absolutely not—I really believe that extra chromosome comes with all his cute and quirky traits. Do I wish I could change his health concerns? Absolutely yes. Wouldn't any mother?

I look forward to the future but whenever Saajan's annual heart appointment comes up, I'm paralysed with fear. Of all the appointments he has, it's the one I still battle with facing. Perhaps as I take myself back to the day when we were on our way to his first heart appointment, I remember how bushy-tailed I was, planning our holiday to Punta Cana, which was just a few weeks away, blissfully oblivious.

Till this day, I have very limited knowledge about his open-heart surgery and his heart defect—ignorant and irresponsible perhaps, but from the moment we heard the consultant's shrilling words, my mind blocked out anything to do with it. It wasn't denial; it was shock. Perhaps even more shocking than receiving his diagnosis of Down's syndrome.

We are so very fortunate that Saajan's heart defect was detected *before* we boarded that plane as the consultant told us very frankly, he may not have made it. The thought sends a shiver down my spine. I have to remind myself to be grateful that it *was* detected beforehand.

Sometimes I take Saajan to his therapies and general check-ups alone, but this one? This one I can't do. Before, I'd attend with Preetam, but now, I prefer not to attend at all. The mum guilt that comes with that is immense. It's usually a two-hour appointment in total with the various tests. The apprehension while waiting is overwhelming for me—especially when I have his beautiful beaming face before my eyes. The guilt washes over me further at the thought of him having to endure that same pain again. I feel helpless that I'm unable to stop it or that perhaps I wasn't able to protect him enough when he was inside me.

During his first surgery, they managed to nip the other side of his heart (one of the complications associated with open-heart surgery) so he now has a leaky valve. We'd hoped it'd resolve within the first-year post-surgery, but unfortunately not. We've been told that for now, the leak is under control, but that there is a chance that Saajan will need open-heart surgery when he's older. For now, I manage to block it. One of the beautiful things that giving birth to my Saajy has taught me is that there is no point in worrying about years ahead when I don't even know what tomorrow holds. Sometimes, I get lost in the day-to-day and the milestones he has to achieve forgetting that the boy has climbed mountains just to be here. He has fought for his life.

Preetam and I make the best team for our little unit —Preetam takes Saajan to his hospital appointments and

I take Saajan to his therapies and manage most of his paperwork. We work together and ensure we support each other when the other waivers. I'm grateful that our personalities complement each other rather than being the same!

The dynamic of our marriage has definitely changed from those initial days of cuddling up on the sofa and enjoying a slower pace of life. With kids comes a great deal of responsibility. With kids with additional needs comes a great deal of urgency. Preetam has shared with me that he wakes up every single day with this thought—"If I died today, would Saajan be okay for life?" Such heavy thoughts but it is his absolute priority that Saajan is always okay, with or without us, as he knows that he will be financially vulnerable as he grows.

Any hurdles we cross, we know that Saajan is the glue that cements us together—no one will ever love our babies the way we love them. Marriage isn't a destination, it's a journey. We've had many ups and downs and faced many challenges and hurdles in our marriage, but we both always say "there is no one else I'd rather be riding this journey with".

As I reflect on the blog post that Preetam wrote when Saajan was first born, it's incredible just how far we have come. Saajan is the absolute apple of all of our eyes and Preetam is besotted by him as he is Arjun. Their bond is indescribable!

Recently, Preetam said, "Harps, we really need to get our wills sorted".

"Don't speak to me about this please, Preetam."
I can't handle the thought of anything happening to
him because I fear how I'd cope without him. He is the
cornerstone of our family—the strength, the organiser,
the rational one. Where I struggle to think of death and
change, he is a realist and will do everything in his power
to prepare for those eventualities. Morbid but real.

As his parents, we are hopeful for Saajan's future and
will fight endlessly for him to get what he needs. We will
be by his side supporting him to achieve his dreams.

We embrace Saajan's fun personality—he is the joker
of the family and his intuition is phenomenal. Even
without speaking many words, he will know exactly
what you are feeling and will respond accordingly. He
always knows when I'm in need of a hug! "Saajan" means
friend—I can't think of a better name for my little guy.
He exhibits so many of the traits I wish we had—living in
the moment, confident and doesn't hold a grudge!

Arjun is a beautiful, caring, strong-willed little boy.
He has his moments, as does any child, but I always reflect
on how much he has had to endure and my heart softens
and tolerance increases (sometimes!). Please don't assume
that an unexpected diagnosis will be devastating to any
other children you have—there will be many beautiful
and enriching lessons. I'm not saying there won't be
challenging moments but isn't that the case with having
siblings anyway?!

Arjun's love for his brother is my greatest strength
during my weakest moments. While Arjun loves Saajan
so fiercely, I know he carries the weight of the world on

his shoulders and worries about things that a typical five-year-old wouldn't because of all that he has witnessed. We pray that their love and relationship continue to thrive. He is so protective, so defensive and so patient. He is also so aware and attentive towards Saajan's needs— we call him Saajan's "thickened water" bodyguard as he is constantly checking that Saajan's water is ok! He is his greatest cheerleader and while he grows and becomes more inquisitive, we will continue to bring them both up full of love, compassion and care. He will often come downstairs in odd socks and tell us he's celebrating Down's syndrome every day because he loves his brother so much. If his friends question why Saajan isn't yet walking, Arjun

Double trouble—Saajan & Arjun

has his reply ready and isn't afraid to share it. He shares it with pride and with no judgement.

The bond that I feared I'd never have with Arjun is there stronger than ever—we are closer than ever and he's definitely a mummy's boy. He continues to be my strength and I love him more than I ever could have imagined from those initial days and months of him entering this world.

I know as the boys get older and the gap widens, there will be further questions. We will continue to teach Arjun, with love and compassion, that it's okay to be different.

When Saajan was born, I had assumed we'd never travel again. I thought he'd have sensory issues and would hate flying, but he does it like a pro. I thought he'd hate being around people, but he's the biggest social butterfly in our family. I thought he'd hate the sand and water, and though it took him time, we've gotten there. We've done over 10 countries in two years. We got to visit my beloved Harmandir Sahib with the boys and both sets of grandparents. It was my wish to return to my safe haven to thank the Almighty for giving me a second chance with Saajan.

One of our trips also included my parents' birth place—Kenya. We decided on doing a family safari at the Masai Mara but I was so nervous, not knowing whether Saajan would get freaked out and panic and, in turn, make lots of noise at the sight of an animal and that I'd not be able to control him. I was left stunned by his behaviour while there—it was more than I could ever have dreamt

Us at Harmandir Sahib to thank God for everything

of. He waved and blew kisses at the animals and he wasn't fazed by the sound of a roaring lion a few metres away; in fact, he roared back! He embraced it; he enjoyed it. We had game drives of up to seven hours long during which he'd fall asleep when he needed to and enjoyed it when he was awake.

On our recent trip to Cape Verde, it was lovely to watch him play with another child doing a regular thing

*Saajan watching the lions in the Masai Mara
while on safari*

and see him playing so beautifully. It was lovely to watch
the little boy's parents encourage their son to play with
Saajan. It was nice to have an open dialogue about Down's
syndrome—I pray this is a glimpse into our future.

As he is growing, it's so nice to see Saajan developing more typical relationships—something that I feared so much when he was born. Children see the world through unfiltered lenses. Parents very much set the narrative on how they view the world.

Seeing Saajan interact with kids from nursery is also wonderful. It gives me hope that the future isn't mundane, it's bright. Children are pure and innocent, so their outlook and approach are very much influenced by the way in which their parents react to those with a difference. This is something I continue to echo on my blog as a reminder for parents.

I know that we really are relying on good fortune for Saajan's future when it comes to his teachers, teaching assistants and therapists—it's a sort of gamble. We've been so fortunate to date! This really worries me but I try and bring my focus back to the here and now. We were fortunate with his keyworker Ashleigh and I feared so much when he moved rooms and got a new keyworker, Toni. Since then, Toni has been my right-hand woman through the second stage of Saajan's nursery life and his development over that time has been incredible.

Toni, through her deep love for Saajan, has shown me I had nothing to fear. He's had a profound impact on her life just like she's had on his and I know that alone will keep our bond going but I was devastated when I found out that she was leaving.

When she handed me a leaving gift for Saajan and I saw that she'd taken the time to get him a personalised beaker and cup, it reinforced just why I'm going to miss her—even in her absence, she's thought about his next milestone—to be able to drink from an open cup. The words she wrote in her card will be etched in my heart forever as a reminder that he is so loved. We pray that every person who walks into Saajan's life could be even half of what Toni had been to him!

And just like that, those fears and anxiety came flooding back except with an even greater force as the gap between Saajan and his peers widens, I fear that his needs will be missed. Relying on good fortune can feel pretty shitty at times—we won't always have control of who will be taking care of Saajan in an educational setting and I fear that the same love that Toni and Ashleigh had for him, which shone through in his development, won't always be there. And I fear how this will impact my child who thrives on patience, kindness and love.

He's doing really well at nursery. He participated in the Christmas concert and, as nervous as I was about other parents looking at him and watching his mannerism, actually, everyone was just interested in their own child! I'll often worry about Saajan's quirks and people staring—thankfully, Preetam is oblivious and reminds me to focus on our own unit and not others.

Seeing Arjun starting school has made me really fear for how we'll cope once Saajan is in school. There is no way he'd be able to keep up. What if he's left out? What if I'm the mum at the school gates that no one wants to speak to because I have a child with additional needs? What if he never gets invited to any parties? I often feel guilty for letting my thoughts slide to Saajan when I should be focusing on Arjun. Then I remind myself of friends like Dina who have made an active effort to ensure their children embrace Saajan and love him for him.

But being as candid as I am, I've shared my feelings with some of the school mums in Arjun's year—many of which will be the same school mums that I will hopefully get to meet when Saajan starts school as they also have younger kids. The kindness and comfort of strangers is greater than I can articulate. Again, it makes me hopeful for the future.

We're living a pretty regular, happy content life. I'd say our biggest current challenge is sometimes communication. Saajan's brain is developed enough to know what he wants but he isn't always able to communicate it and that can be frustrating for him. I have to stop myself from getting frustrated by reminding myself how frustrating it must be for him being trapped in his own mind without having all the right tools to be able to communicate, but we're working on it!

The truth is, there are things Saajan can't do, but the bottom line is love conquers all. His worth is not tied to his ability. He is worthy just being him.

Watching our families celebrate and shower Saajan and Arjun with so much love has instilled us with confidence too. One of my fears had been that Saajan would be rejected by the family. I never in my wildest dreams had imagined that he'd be the most fiercely loved and protected. Watching my father-in-law interact with Saajan, taking so much time, love and patience to teach him new skills, from gardening to learning new words, is beautiful. How my mother-in-law excitedly takes them on new adventures from cooking new things to taking the bus and how she yearns for both boys when they're not with them brings me comfort. I am forever indebted to them. He is literally the centre of attention in any room he enters. My parents continue to pray for the boys endlessly. Watching the boys scoot around my dad for fruit time reminds me of my childhood. My mum encouraging the boys to pray also reminds me of my childhood. The support of our family held us up during the storm. I am forever grateful for our siblings—Indy's favourite phrase is "he's mad cute" when playing with Saajan, he's Arjun's giant best friend; to Mané fighting my mother-in-law for a Saajy cuddle, to watching Sarvun, Saajan and Arjun grow together. Harv has felt inspired by Saajan and has decided she'd like to pursue a career working with kids with additional needs and has recently secured a position fulfilling that dream. Goov continues to remind me of all the positives anytime I waiver. With an army of support behind us, I need not fear our future! And such is our fortune that our siblings went on to marry husbands and wives who champion our boys just as much as they do! Because of Saajan, we celebrate life more intensely than we ever have before.

When I pause and reflect on my immediate unit, and by that, I'm referring to Preetam, Arjun, Saajan and myself, there isn't a single thing that feels like it's missing—I feel complete, I feel happy, I feel content, I feel overwhelmed with joy and gratitude and I feel blessed when we are in our little bubble. Sometimes, I still hold my breath—I'm

Saajan, Arjun and their cousin Sarvun
who is a day younger than Saajan!

Our army of support—our precious family

Our family rocking odd socks for
World Down's Syndrome Day

almost too scared to feel happy in fear that something "bad" will suddenly happen, but as time is passing, I'm learning to view hurdles as just that—hurdles. They don't define our happiness. I feel hopeful, positive and excited for the future!

I am grateful that he was born in a day and age where people who are differently abled are celebrated and included in mainstream media as opposed to being locked up in mental institutions as they were just 30 years ago. Major companies such as Benefit Cosmetics, River Island and Primark have featured models with Down's syndrome. It's a major breakthrough to challenge society's perceptions and to show that those with Down's syndrome are also beautiful and able.

As for me, when I look back at the person I first was when entering motherhood, I barely recognise myself. I no longer sit at home watching the CCTV when I'm alone with the kids—I have surrendered that fear! I'm still apprehensive about taking the kids out of the car when we get home—especially now that there are two and I am unable to take them both out at the same time! I'm great at giving *both* the boys a bath alone now! I'm okay with co-sleeping with my kids—I was one of those mums who would never have dreamt of co-sleeping but actually, my kids have opened my eyes and heart—they won't be little forever and while I can, I intended on giving them as much love, security and affection as they want!

For the times when I do feel overwhelmed, I have the familiarity, the scent, the cosy carpet that feels like you're walking on a bed of cotton wool, the snack cupboard overflowing, and the peace I find at my parents' home is still the same as it did when I was a little girl. I am transported back to my childhood anytime I visit—I find ultimate peace in their attic where they have a prayer room. The stillness and silence make me feel grounded and connected.

I've learnt to appreciate the beauty of individuality—I have two children being brought up in the same house but with such different personalities. I value their unique qualities just like I valued my sisters and my own growing up. I look forward to watching them grow into the men that they will become.

When I have an anxious moment thinking about the future, I limit that feeling and remind myself that "this too shall pass". I'll find stolen minutes to sit and teleport myself to a place of peace—that is free of fear, free of apprehension, free of doubt. To my safe haven— Sri Harmandir Sahib. I place the cream-coloured shawl, gifted to me by my dad especially for meditating, and sit in front of a beautiful picture of Sri Harmandir Sahib that my parents gifted me when we moved in to our home. I close my eyes and let my mind and soul float into bliss.

"I'm sitting by the glistening sarovar with my beautiful golden home standing tall at its centre. It is the home that houses and unearths so many of my deep emotions.

It's early in the morning and the noise of the hustle and bustle is muted. I'm surrounded by tranquillity. It's cool and breezy but I feel a warmth radiating inside me and around me—it comes as soon as I place the cream-coloured shawl over my shoulders. It's the protective hand of Guru Nanak Dev Ji as I sit and listen to the echo of the beautiful kirtan from inside. I feel calm. I feel uplifted from the chaos beneath me. I feel safe. I feel warm. I feel shielded. I can see beyond this chaos. There is stillness—I can feel and hear my heartbeat. It is in sync with the harmonious melody I hear echoing from inside my beautiful golden home. I am laced with love and hope. My Guru is with me. All will be okay.

I open my eyes; my heart yearns to go back."

They told me they were sorry but no one told me how much joy he would bring.

They told me I'd have lots of appointments but no one told me how much more time we'd get to spend as a family.

They told me he'd be slow but no one told me how much determination he'd have.

They told me things would be frustrating but no one told me how much more rewarding they would be.

They told me he'd be different but no one told me how loved he'd be.

To know that our little boy has changed the fate of other families is incredible.

While I didn't take comfort in some of the professionals who, I remind myself, have no first-hand experience of parenting a child with Down's syndrome, who I did take great comfort in were the other amazing mothers who connected with me through social media who were further down in their journey and who held my hand really tightly and told me it was going to be ok; that I wouldn't always feel this way.

They never broke their promise.

They knew the reality and they promised it really isn't that bad. I took comfort in them because they provided me with a light at the end of the tunnel. They continue to be my light while we have become the light for others. I am grateful for technology connecting me with our present network—I don't feel lonely on this journey. I am surrounded by an entirely new family, full of love, hope and support. Who could have predicted what BabyBrainMemoirs.com would become when I hit "publish" on my first blog post all the way in 2014 and how my story, our story, would unfold?

I often get asked the below questions via the blog and wanted to summarise my answers based on my own experiences here:

1. As medical professionals, what are your tips and suggestions for delivering a Down's syndrome diagnosis to parents?

Based on our experience, and the experience of so many families that I've spoken to, the delivery of a Down's syndrome diagnosis very much has a part to play in the initial narrative that is formed around the diagnosis.

- **Be mindful of your choice of words:** at whichever stage you are delivering the diagnosis, your words WILL have a huge impact. When you hear the word "risk" what springs to mind? Danger. Red. Escape. Using the words "high risk" places an immediate fear in the person receiving the news influencing their decision and feelings. Human nature is to protect ourselves from risk. Does Saajan seem dangerous or scary to you? The use of the word "chance" is more appropriate!

- **Read the info you share:** I was handed a heartless leaflet moments after receiving the diagnosis. When I opened the FIRST page it told me that my baby had a 15% increased chance of leukaemia. It set me in to a panicked frenzy and an even darker place especially as they struggled to draw bloods from Saajan and I feared the worst. It would have been more beneficial to have been sign-posted to real life accounts and charities such as The Positive About Down Syndrome (PADS) and Wouldn't Change A Thing (WCAT) charities.

- **Don't comment on something that you have not experienced yourself:** I was told by some that our lives were never going to be the same again with a pitiful glance which insinuated that our lives were doomed. It instilled panic and fear in me. Instead, put parents in touch with families that have first-hand experience. It was these families who in fact had first-hand experience that took me out of my deep dark hole! Be mindful of parents mirroring your reaction as before they have a chance to process the news, they may base their feelings on your reaction. This can also contribute to PND. The Positive About Down's Syndrome Charity has curated a book called "#NobodyToldMe" which is a collection of personal experiences written by young people with Down's syndrome and their friends and family. It challenges the outdated perceptions and attitudes towards those with Down's syndrome by showing the *reality*—you may spot us in it! I'd highly recommend all hospitals have a copy of this book to hand to share with parents that may be receiving a diagnosis.
- **Don't say "I'm sorry", instead congratulate them!** Using the word "sorry" can make the person receiving

the words feel as though something really catastrophic has happened. What are you sorry for? Yes, life is a little different, but why should different be seen as bad?

Your tone, choice of words and the information you share influences those precious first moments for parents—a memory that lasts forever.

2. How can I support our family or friends when they have just received a Down's syndrome diagnosis?

As you have probably gathered from reading this far, the way in which family and friends reacted, played a big part in how I processed the news. While I appreciate that it's important to not be led by external factors in life, when you're feeling vulnerable, often people look to their loved ones for hope. While I appreciate the *intention* isn't to cause any offence or pain, the tongue is like a double-edged sword and your words could make all the difference! Here are some useful pointers based on our experience:

DON'T say...

- **Didn't you know before? Didn't you get the test done?:** this isn't at all helpful and actually insinuates all types of awful things. It insinuates that perhaps if we had known, the outcome would have been different.
- **I wouldn't be able to do it:** this is patronising and sounds like "thank God it's you and not me". What

choice do parents have other than to be strong and ride it?

- **Is there a cure?:** in short, no! It isn't a disease. It's just an extra copy of chromosome 21.
- **Life isn't going to be what you expected:** don't comment on this unless you have first-hand experience. Passing negative comments could have devastating consequences on the parents' mental health.
- **Special children are born to special parents:** it's patronising. There is nothing "special" about us. We are just regular parents, doing what all parents do— trying our best.
- **He/she doesn't look like they have Down's syndrome, is it mild?:** you may think that this is being kind but actually it's not. Accept the child for who they are and whatever comes with that. You either have Down's syndrome or you don't. The level of learning difficulty is in no way linked to physical features.
- **I'm so sorry:** what for?

Instead…

- **Congratulate them!** They've just had a baby!
- **Be inclusive and show their newborn unconditional love.**
- **Use the words "we" instead of "you"**—the power of this was immense for me; Sav has always made me feel less alone and has meant it!
- **Check in on them and show them that you are there.** Don't just say it, show them even if they don't

respond to your messages or answer your calls for a little while.

- **Start convos about Down's syndrome.** This has spoken volumes for us to see those that have gone the extra mile to help make the world a more accepting place for people like our son.
- **Tell them you're excited to learn more.** Sharing that you're planning on being a part of this journey with them will make it a less lonely time for them. But only say it if you're planning on sticking around for the ride! Insincerity is not cool.

Most of all, love them, support them and just be there.

3. How should we educate our children on embracing those with additional needs?

Firstly, thank you to those who proactively want to educate their children and secondly, I pray the world has more of you because you give parents like me hope and faith!...

- **Education most definitely starts at home** and the most important thing to note is that our children will follow the example that we set. Model the right behaviours and they'll follow!
- **Don't shush your children away,** instead feed their inquisitive nature and—allow them to feel comfortable to ask questions. Ask their parents if you're unsure.

- **Model the right behaviours** and your children will follow. For example, treat those with additional needs the same as you would any other child by saying hello.
- **Encourage your children to celebrate difference—** be it colour, race, gender or ability! Be inclusive, for example in the books you read to them, in the TV programmes they may watch, when you're organising play dates or sending out birthday party invites.
- **Encourage your children to see beyond the disability** by talking about regular things such as what the child may be good t or what their likes and dislikes are.
- **Don't show pity, show love, kindness and acceptance.**
- **If your child notices a difference, don't pretend that it doesn't exist.** It's about *seeing* difference and *choosing* to treat everyone as equal despite those differences. Encourage your children to help those that may need a little helping hand.

Remember, those with additional needs also want to be loved, accepted and shown kindness just like you and me.

I continue to write my blog despite wondering whether I'd ever write again. It's strange to think that I am now too that mum who offers a safe hand and space for mothers receiving a new diagnosis. "One day, you will tell your story of how you've overcome what you're going through now, and it will become part of someone else's survival guide" (Brene Brown). I'm grateful to have liberal parents who support my open writing—not something typical of South Asian families. My parents are my greatest cheerleaders when it comes to raising awareness and sharing.

Recently, I was having a clear-out upstairs and I came across a stack of pictures and an unfilled scrapbook that I'd put aside. They were the pictures from Saajan's open-heart surgery. I'd taken hundreds of them during that time, purposefully, because I wanted to have them to be able to look back on, to reflect on. As painful as it is to look at some of those images, it's important for me to be able to reawaken some of the emotions we felt then to appreciate where we are now. I had left the pictures there because I didn't feel ready to look at them. Yet, stumbling upon them today, I decided it was time. I cried, I laughed, and I fell to my knees as I sobbed uncontrollably at the immense love I feel for Saajan—something that I was just learning to do back then, and the fear of losing him… I prayed.

I filled the book with the images. What amazed me, on reflection, was the balance in those pictures—heartbreak, happiness, fear, hope, desperation, faith. For every heart-breaking picture, there's an image that uplifts me, be it a picture of Arjun on an adventure with his masis, which reminds me that I thought about him too at a time when my heart felt shattered, or be it a picture of a cake slice which reminds me that I listened to the advice of the nurses to go and get some much needed me time whilst they took care of Saajan or be it a picture of my sisters with us because it reminds me how much love we are surrounded by—even though we have faced many hurdles, My Guru has never ever failed to provide us with an appropriate support network, angels in disguise. For that, I am forever grateful. I look back through our journey and I feel proud that we have hundreds of pictures that don't paint a dreary image but ones that show the lows *and* the highs and how we managed to find silver linings even when we were staring the prospect of death straight in the face. This book isn't just about documenting Saajan's new lease of life; it's also a celebration of us as a unit and how far we came during that time.

I am forever grateful to God for carrying us through such a heart-wrenching time. Looking back, I'm not sure how we did it. We had no choice. Our kids were, and will always be our strength, and faith will always be our anchor in any storm.

Twelve scans including two anomalies and two nuchal, six different sonographers, a screening result of one in 100,000… we hit the jackpot. Saajan wasn't a "risk", he was a *chance*. How can I question whether this was meant to be? There is no shadow of doubt in my mind. It *was* meant to be but I just needed time to accept it. Saajan has changed our life positively in so many ways—we take day trips to the seaside, we embrace the slower pace and we celebrate the smallest of milestones. I'm such a strong believer in God and one thing that never changed through all of this was my faith—I never question when God does good for me, so why would I question this? To me, He only does what's right for us. Perhaps it was because we'd had so many scans by so many different sonographers, there wasn't a single person I could blame. Perhaps it was because our chances were so slim and I began to compare it to the chances of winning the lottery as Mrs G had said. I believe in life after death and I believe that perhaps in a past life, Saajan took great care of me, and now in this life, I'm being given the honour to take care of him. Who knows?! I choose to see him as the paper chain to my plant like that Christmas when I was 15 years old.

As ashamed as I am to admit it, I was that person who was blinded by the label. And now, I'm here to challenge it. According to Mencap, there are approximately 351,000 children aged 0-17 with a learning disability in the UK. It's time to change the narrative. The blog has now become a platform for actively raising awareness for Down's syndrome as well as PND—my purpose in life has become far greater than I ever could have imagined—all thanks to two little boys who have crowned me "mummy". My greatest goal is to help change the narrative, especially in the South Asian community—we've appeared on The Sikh Channel and other media outlets to spread awareness and I work with our local Gurdwara to foster a more open and inclusive environment for those with SEN.

We will continue to face challenges with both of our children—that's what parenthood is about. Through those challenges, we find growth. I look at both sets of our parents now and even though we've grown up, they still face their challenges with us!

Despite the extra routine appointments which happen annually now, weekly SALT appointments and monthly physio appointments which I class the same as what we'd be doing baby-group-wise, our lives feel pretty regular. We've just grown with Saajan and his schedule. It doesn't feel weird or alien to us; it's just our norm.

Saajan's resilience inspires me every single day. He tackles his appointments and whatever life throws his way with a huge smile and with so much courage. He loves hospital appointments, isn't fazed by needles at his annual blood test and will happily play ball at the doctors! I often miss my Suzi Thai Ji—Saajan's smile, courage and zest for life reminds me so much of her. She would have adored him had she had the chance to meet him.

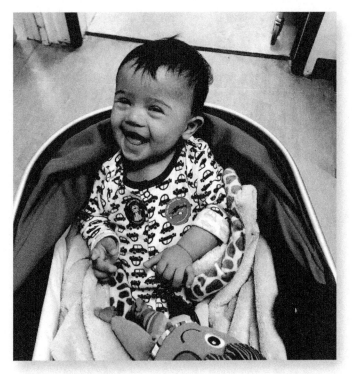

Saajan during one of his hospital appointments

We are letting our beautiful boys guide us through life, and, despite the challenges, we are really enjoying our journey. I know we will have many hurdles to cross, but, as a family, we will conquer every single one; one day at a time.

I don't view Saajan's diagnosis as a disaster anymore. He has taught us so much in such a short space of time. He has enriched our lives more than I could ever have imagined the day he was born. He's changed who I am completely; he's given us a real purpose in life. That purpose was always there, I just needed to lift the veil of judgement to be able to see it.

Celebrating World Down's Syndrome Day with the family

Our life is full of chaos, but when I come home and have my babies snuggle up to me like little lion cubs, I remind myself that there isn't a single thing that I'd change about our lives!

Looking back on myself pre-marriage and pre-kids, I feel like a very different woman with the same core. Navigating the realms of reality has taught me that life isn't always simple, but through it, I can still find my own happiness. Saajan was my storm that turned into my brightest sunshine and here I am living a refreshed version of my fairy-tale life with my husband, two children and an unexpected diagnosis!

Us at Saajan's second birthday party

Useful Websites/Resources

Sparkles: https://www.facebook.com/SparklesCharity/

Positive About Down Syndrome Charity:
https://positiveaboutdownsyndrome.co.uk/

Wouldn't Change a Thing Charity:
https://www.wouldntchangeathing.org/

Emma Hopkins Consultancy:
https://www.facebook.com/emmahopkinsconsultancy